The Bulldog Track

The Bulldog Track

PETER PHELPS

Published in Australia and New Zealand in 2018
by Hachette Australia
(an imprint of Hachette Australia Pty Limited)
Level 17, 207 Kent Street, Sydney NSW 2000
www.hachette.com.au

10 9 8 7 6 5 4 3 2 1

A catalogue record for this book is available from the National Library of Australia

ISBN: 978 0 7336 3977 7 (paperback)

Cover design by Christabella Designs
Cover photographs courtesy of the author and Shutterstock
Text design by Kirby Jones
Typeset in Sabon LT Std by Kirby Jones
Printed and bound in Australia by McPherson's Printing Group

The paper this book is printed on is certified against the Forest Stewardship Council® Standards. McPherson's Printing Group holds FSC® chain of custody certification SA-COC-005379. FSC® promotes environmentally responsible, socially beneficial and economically viable management of the world's forests.

In loving memory of two good men –
Thomas Henry Phelps, my grandfather
and George Thomas Phelps OAM, my father.

Here it is, Dad.

'Longer, higher, steeper, wetter, colder and rougher than Kokoda.'

Peter Ryan, author of *Fear Drive My Feet*

Contents

Author's Note

All families have stories that weave into the fabric that defines how each member views themselves. My grandfather's wartime experiences in New Guinea, along with those of my father and his sisters back home, have become part of what carrying the Phelps name means to me – resilience, the importance of family, the loyalty of mates and an optimism that can carry you through the worst of times.

Growing up, I knew bits and pieces about Pop's time in the New Guinea Highlands during World War II. He taught pidgin English to my cousins and me, and he would entertain us with stories of this mysterious other place. For a kid it sounded like my grandfather went goldmining in the jungle with Tarzan. The scariest, most fun and adventurous time. We were only ever told the good stories, of course. Nothing about enemy air attacks or cannibals on the trail, or the death and disease that surrounded the men on my grandfather's journey. I discovered all this and more many years later in my research. My dad and aunts would also share what they knew. It was only in recent times, as my father's health declined, that I realised I needed to write down what had happened to Tom Phelps in those years, before his story was lost forever. I also needed to capture on paper the way his absence affected his children; specifically, my father, George. This paternal absence was one of the high prices of the Depression and of World War I and World War II as men were forced to leave their families in order to fight or to find work.

My father was on the road for most of his working life, whether it was inspecting pubs as an engineer for Tooth's Brewery or fly-in/fly-out trips when he himself worked in New Guinea, commissioned by the army as a supervisor in a multi-million-dollar Army Expansion Program. Dad had sworn to Mum that he would never spend more than a week away from his family. He always loved his old man and knew his absence was for the benefit of his wife and kids, but he would never forget his feeling of longing and abandonment and wouldn't let it visit his own family. So, Dad brought my mother, sister and me to live in New Guinea for the three years of his tenure.

When my family returned, Dad would never miss a footy match, swimming meet, surf carnival or theatre production I was in and this has impacted my approach to fatherhood with my daughters. He would always be there for his kids as I am with mine today.

Pop and the men on the Bulldog Track weren't soldiers, so when they came back no one gathered their oral histories. And when he came home, Pop, like many others, at first didn't want to talk about the things he'd seen and the hardships he'd faced. He wanted to get on with things and not look back.

His recollections came in fits and starts, and it took many years for the pieces to slot together and for truths to be revealed. Pop's connection to New Guinea was forged when he arrived in the Highlands to work for the Bulolo Gold Dredging Company (BGD Co.) in 1939. Even after such a harrowing exit the first time round – one that I will reveal in the pages that follow – Tom returned several times to work in what would become Papua New Guinea and would often visit Bulolo locals who, he told his grandsons (including me), had saved his and his mates' lives on the journey that forms the basis of this book.

I am not a historian. This book is not a concise history of chronologically factual happenings that occurred after the Japanese invasion of New Guinea and the evacuation of the Bulolo township. It is a family memoir of rememberings and imaginings that spin off from key moments in the lives of my grandfather and father.

I am an actor and so I have spent years bringing to life other people's stories by using the truth of them to create the moods, actions and responses that can convey that life to others. This is what I have tried to do in *The Bulldog Track*. At times I have condensed and sped up events to highlight the key moments. I have tried to banish my present-day judgements in the telling to capture the authenticity of the times, and in doing so I have employed the language my Pop used, which was commonplace in Australia and New Guinea in the 1930s and 1940s. The terms 'bois', 'Japs', 'natives' and 'waitmen' might not resonate in today's parlance but they were the descriptors everyone used back then. This story is informed by the knowledge I gained from my grandfather, my dad and my aunts; from research I undertook at the State Library of New South Wales; and through my contact with other families whose relatives trekked the Bulldog at the time; all this raw memory and material helped me to imagine what happened in those key moments. My own time in Papua New Guinea has also bled into these pages. I began my first two years of school in Port Moresby, school shoes optional, and would often go with my mother and sister to Dad's workplace at the army barracks or fly into towns around the country. We would visit the town of Bulolo and the goldfields where my grandfather lived and worked.

However, this book is not a work of fiction. The truth of this story lies in the emotional journey of my grandfather and my father – and of my own life's work – and it is a tribute to the resilience and strength that saw my grandfather survive, and his family hold together while he was gone. It is a tribute to all those who survived the Bulldog Track.

Peter Phelps
Sydney, 2018

Introduction

Under a full moon at Edie Creek, near Bulolo in the New Guinea Highlands, late at night on 4 March 1942, my grandfather might have heard or even said the following sentence: '*Mipela bai kirapim bilong mipela hat wokabaut.*' It means: 'We will start our hardest journey now.'

Pop had a good handle on Tok Pisin, or what he and his mates knew as pidgin English. Years later, as children, my cousins and I used to love learning the words and phrases he taught us. 'How you read it is how you say it,' he always told us, 'so have fun saying it out loud.'

Mipela bai kirapim bilong mipela hat wokabaut.
We will start our hardest journey now.

And they did.

* * *

The Bulldog Track is the story of my grandfather Tom Phelps; and the story of his son, my father, George. It is a story they deserve to have written, and one that I need to tell.

Forty-one days after the Japanese attack on Pearl Harbor announced that nation's entry into World War II, and just two weeks after the Japanese bombed Darwin, a smaller but just as lethal fleet from the same Hawaiian attack that started the war in the Pacific, strafed and bombed the mining town of my grandfather. This was the catalyst for the Australian military to destroy the town in a scorched earth destruction of Bulolo, leaving nothing for the impending Japanese invaders. And nothing left for the European residents. A planned evacuation by plane from the neighbouring town of Wau (pronounced 'Wow') was aborted by yet another bombing of that town and the destruction of all aircraft. To quote my grandfather: 'Again our hopes were dashed by being bombed twice in a week.' It became the trigger for Tom and a group of 200 or so other civilians based in the Highlands of New Guinea – goldminers, tradesmen, professionals and local carriers – to set out on a momentous trek along what came to be known as the Bulldog Track. They were fleeing the

Japanese army, which was now pressing down through New Guinea. My grandfather again: 'We hatched our plans to go overland by this unknown trail in the hope of reaching the coast of Papua.'

Most of the party were unarmed. Some were old, and some sick, but all of them were unprepared for the wild rapids, the impregnable jungle – in which tribes known to indulge in cannibalism resided – the unseeable enemy, the air raids, the disease and the deaths. It was a journey similar to that made by Australian servicemen on the Kokoda Track later in 1942, but the Bulldog Track was – according to Peter Ryan – 'longer, higher, steeper, wetter, colder and rougher'.

The Australians on Tom's epic trek – all of them too old or unfit to enlist in the military – knew of the atrocities committed on behalf of the Japanese Emperor as the enemy advanced south. Tom and his mates believed an invasion was inevitable.

This part of New Guinea was, at the time, an Australian territory. As the Aussies of Bulolo saw it, the Japs had already busted down Australia's back fence and were poised to kick in the door of their native land. The members of this small community weren't going to hang around and wait to be killed. They would try to reach safety the only way they could: by foot, through some of the most rugged terrain on Earth.

My dad, George Phelps, was ten years old in September 1939, when his father left for New Guinea. George was bitter at what he saw as his father's abandonment of his family. Tom had left to work as a goldminer and carpenter, not to join up to defend his country. What's more, his father wouldn't be around to watch George – who was obsessed with rugby league – fulfil his ambition of playing representative football.

Despite his anger, George promised his father that he would be the man of the house for the next three years (the length of Tom's contract). He pledged to look out for his mother and three sisters.

At the time, neither Tom nor George realised they would soon be tested like never before.

* * *

Tom Phelps's eldest child, my Aunty Joy, is the family historian. I began my research whilst staying on her and her partner Joan's coffee plantation in the northern New South Wales town of Woombah (pronounced 'Womba', population 844). Joy rediscovered Tom's photos from the time and I have included some of these photos in this book. Each time I flip through them I am amazed at how a camera and its film stock made it out of whitewater rapids and knee-high mud and torrential rain and all sorts of adverse conditions to, thankfully, survive so the images can make it onto these pages.

I couldn't find out which one of Tom's sixteen other miner mates lugged the camera along for the ride, but surely it would have been a prized possession. A favourite shot, and one that typifies that Aussie spirit in the face of adversity, is one of the smiling men aboard their newly handmade raft, moored to a riverbank by vines, posing for the camera as if they were Boy Scouts recreating Huckleberry Finn's raft trip down the Mississippi River. I believe it was my grandfather who took the shot from the riverbank, as at this point the miners had split up into groups of four, five or six. In the shot are Pop's group of six, minus Pop.

I did mini detective work like this numerous times throughout the book.

The only other remaining physical evidence of Tom Phelps's journey is a rudimentary diary written with his carpenter's pencil onto what was once a white round-domed, canvas covered pith helmet. He began with the title at the crown on top in capitals – 'WALK ACROSS NEW GUINEA' – and made entries in a spiral pattern until there was no further room to write just as the men had reached the Yule Island Mission near the end of their trek. He also created a map written on baking paper, which records the names of his fellow trekkers – those who survived and those who did not – where burials took place, and every camp along the trail.

I kept Pop's map, diary and helmet close to me while I wrote his story. These artefacts – his handwriting and his drawings – travelled with him, on his head, in his pack and in his pockets. I can picture him settling in at a new camp after a nine-hour hike, a feed and a communal chat about the next stage of the journey, then jotting down the day's events. Now, more than seventy-five years later, all the witnesses have gone to their graves, but Pop's possessions speak to me. The inscription on his helmet, made somewhere around the halfway point of the journey – where the cloudforest meets the Eloa River and becomes the Lakekamu River, at an abandoned mine camp called Bulldog – is typically simple: 'fished native style ... hunted game with new natives fleeing Japs too'. It's all written in his beautiful looping handwriting.

I built on these snippets with morsels picked up from my research, and a lot of time spent at the State Library of New South Wales. Information was minimal. The battles, skirmishes, manoeuvres, personnel, dates and all things military were well documented, both at the time and later, by great journalists writing for Australian readers – Chester Wilmot, Osmar White and George Johnston, to name just three. But the experiences of civilians in New Guinea at the time are lesser known. In large part, they remained silent.

Pop did write one extraordinary letter about his time travelling the Bulldog Track. He wrote in response to an article in the paper published nine days previously, which was written almost exclusively about the army engineers, road builders and native labourers who, phenomenally, created the Bulldog Road from the Bulldog Track in what Australian head honcho General Sir Thomas Blamey said ranked among the 'great Army engineering feats of history'. It became a vital supply route for the battles ahead with the Japanese, including the Kokoda campaign. It was the highest road ever constructed in Australian territory, at 9857 feet and earned its Chief Engineer, Lieutenant Colonel WJ Reinhold, the OBE and the Military Cross. The army gave the road an alternative name – the Reinhold Highway. But the miners who first set a white foot on it would never call it that.

There was only passing mention in the piece of the evacuated civilian miners and no mention as to how they achieved their extraordinary feat. Many of them were consulted by the army upon reaching safety to gain information, including my grandfather, whose map and diary were studied and given back to him. Pop felt he and his mates and the natives 'to whom most of us owe our lives' (he writes in his letter) should be recognised and in his quiet and subtle way he stated his case. I find in my grandfather's letter, in his voice, how underplayed and reticent this character trait of the Australian man was at the time and how so often the men who returned home said little or nothing of their experiences, whether they were soldiers or civilians.

The letter was addressed to the editor of the *Sydney Morning Herald*, and published in that newspaper on 29 May 1944.

> Sir—
>
> The article by Edward Axford (*SMH*, 20/5/'44), on the building of the Bulldog Road, made known the part played by the men who blazed the trail from Wau and Edie Creek to the Papuan coast by way of Bulldog and the Lakekamu River. Being one of the original party who left Edie Creek at 11 p.m. on March 4, 1942, I can fully substantiate all he says in regard to the hardships endured. I was working on the Bulolo goldfields when the Japanese attacked

New Guinea by air on January 21. They destroyed our company's three planes on the ground at Bulolo, making our evacuation by air impossible. Two days later we proceeded by road to Wau in the hope of being evacuated by air. Again our hopes were dashed by being bombed twice in a week. Now hopelessly cut off from Port Moresby and our own people, we moved up the mountain to Edie Creek. It was from this place that we hatched our plans to go overland by this unknown trail in the hope of reaching the coast of Papua. So we set out a few nights later with very little food and a few of the natives, to whom most of us owe our lives. I should also like to express my gratitude to Dr Giblin, an elderly man, who did everything possible, under terrible conditions, for the sick and injured. We eventually reached the coast very much the worse for wear, I having lost 4st on the journey. We then walked 60 miles down the beach to Yule Island, and later by schooner to Port Moresby, where we gave all the necessary information to the authorities which probably prompted them to build the road. The task they performed can only be appreciated by those who travelled the trail through this country.

THOMAS PHELPS

Punchbowl

This letter was the only first-hand account of the Bulldog Track journey I have seen. It was the inspiration to tell this story and it's my determined aim, Pop, to let a few more than your fellow travellers appreciate this epic journey.

CHAPTER 1

Bulolo Bound

My family has had a connection to Papua New Guinea ever since Tom Phelps arrived in the Owen Stanley Ranges towards the end of September 1939, two weeks after Hitler invaded Poland. He had come to work for the Bulolo Gold Dredging Company (BGD Co.) as a carpenter and goldminer.

The pioneers of goldmining in this area – men such as Cecil Levien, William 'Shark Eye' Park and Jack Nettleton – knew how to entice an international workforce. They made the town of Bulolo as much like home as possible for their expat workers, most of whom came from Australia, New Zealand or the United Kingdom. In 1934, the newly arrived Administrator of the Mandated Territory of New Guinea, Brigadier General Walter McNicoll, observed: 'Bulolo is an amazing place.

Less than four years ago, impenetrable jungle; today a well planned and well established township ... A more striking example of careful and skilful planning and successful execution can hardly be imagined.'

Goldmining done on an industrial scale in New Guinea involved extremely tough working conditions, isolation, a confronting cultural difference and adverse weather, so keeping their employees socially and physically content was the only way the mine owners could ensure they had a consistent workforce, which was critical to a well-functioning mine. And so they did. Bulolo's 330 'Europeans' didn't need to go outside of their purpose-built township. Everything required for comfortable Western living was grown there or flown in.

At sixteen, Tom had enlisted to serve in World War I, but on the day in 1914 he signed his forms, took his medical and was given an Australian Imperial Force service number – 82949 – his mother, Margaret, hauled him out of the recruiting office by the ear, probably to the laughter of his mates bound for the European slaughterhouses. She scolded the recruiting officers for signing up underage lads. The Phelps women have never been backward in going forward.

Twenty-five years later, as the clouds of war hovered above Europe once more, Tom was again unable to enlist, this time on medical grounds. While working on a building site in 1938, his foot had been crushed and became gangrenous as a result of the black dye from his sock infecting the wound. My dad once told me how he remembered seeing the poison rise towards his father's heart. The doctors had wanted to amputate, but were met with a strong refusal. 'You'll amputate my head before you take my foot off,' Tom swore at the medical men. My hard-as-nails grandmother, who similarly dismissed all medical advice, managed to get Tom up and running again with love and ichthyol – black ointment.

If the Sydney doctors had had their way and amputated Tom's foot, he would never have gone to New Guinea as a carpenter at the goldmines. Yet if he had been fit, he would most likely have joined his mates and enlisted – and he may well have seen action on another track, 130 miles to the south, which ran from the Highlands town of Kokoda to Port Moresby.

After Tom recovered, his bad leg hampered his employment chances for a while. Times were tough, and he had mouths to feed – his wife, Rose, and four children, George, Joy, Shirley and Ann. When a mate told Tom that working for the BGD Co. could earn him as much money in a week as he could make in two months in Sydney, he made the fateful decision to sign a contract to live and work in the mystical Highlands of New Guinea. Rose would be able to pick up a regular cheque at BGD Co.'s office on the fourth floor of Shell House on Carrington Street, Sydney.

And so Tom Phelps left Punchbowl and travelled to Bulolo in late September 1939, his goldmining contract and his carpentry tools in hand, ready for a three-year stint on the goldfields. World War II had commenced only a couple of months earlier, but at that stage it was confined to Europe. Tom's arrival in the Highlands came only six years after that of the first 'waitmen' – the Western adventurers and prospectors who appeared out of the jungle trails to make contact with a Highlands population of around 750,000 people. As Tim Flannery has written, 'This was the last time in the history of our planet that such a vast, previously unknown civilisation was to come into contact with the west.'

Tom didn't rave much to Rose and the family in his letters and rare telegrams about the relative luxury of the joint he found himself in, but he could have. At the time he alighted from Bertie Heath's Junkers G31 transport plane from Port Moresby, Bulolo already had a sports club and a golf club, cricket pitches and a 600-yard rifle range. The settlement had teams in many sports, including table tennis, billiards and the less strenuous but more stressful poker. They would compete against players from the other Highlands town, Wau, which sat nineteen miles upriver at an altitude 1247 feet higher than Bulolo, and against the northern coastal towns of Salamaua and Lae. The mining company itself flew the sports teams to their away matches. Bulolo also had a library with reading rooms, a theatre and a cinema where movies were shown on Wednesday and Saturday nights. Sailing regattas were held on disused dredge ponds, and night tennis was played on floodlit courts. Three swimming pools were fed by natural springs, and there were also six bowling greens.

All this for 330 miners and tradesmen, medical staff and their families.

A refrigeration plant had been built in Bulolo early on, in 1932; less than a year earlier, no one in the district had ever seen ice. So, fresh meat, fish and veggies were always on hand. And the weekly tonnage of Foster's Lager airlifted in – on the freight planes named 'Peter', 'Paul' and 'Pat', and captained by either Bertie Heath or Les Ross – made sure the place was never dry.

Around a third of the miners had their families with them. The mine owners were always willing to accommodate this if it kept a man on the job. Tom had asked Rose to come with him, but she'd flatly refused. The fact that the kids' education would be interrupted, combined with her fear of the unknown and the 'primitive', meant the idea was too much for her. So, Tom lived with the bachelor workers, three blokes to a house.

For many among its white population, Bulolo offered a far more luxurious existence than they'd been used to at home. Less salubrious, yet still very liveable, were the native labourers' huts of local timber and thatched roofing, which were built on the fringes of the township. The Highlanders' original villages lay in the uncleared jungle a little further on, and almost all of the 12,000 natives of the district would come and go. The mining towns injected more funds and trading options into their village than would have been the case had the waitman never come.

CHAPTER 2

Bulolo Gold

Tom never looked at his Hartford Lever wristwatch when working on his wooden creations. That would be too much like being on his shift at work. His work was as a full-time goldminer and carpenter for the company, and it was the reason he was so far from his family. When he toiled as a goldminer on the conveyer belts and turbines and water cannons and sluices and the massive, moving machinery of those eight monolithic dredges that floated a quarter of a mile and back in a year on the Bulolo River, he'd watch the clock. All the men did. Just like those who toiled at the tailings on the riverbank and cleared the surrounding jungle of growth that some swore they could see growing before them. Work accompanied by the non-stop steel-on-steel, steel-on-rock clanking and slamming twenty-four hours a day that echoed all over the ridges and deep valleys and through the town day and night.

For those full-timers constantly oiling metal parts that were in unceasing motion, it was always about time. Smoko time, eight-hour bundy on and off time. First beer time. Sleep time. Then came the swim club and activities scheduled at the Bulolo Sports Club. Billiards. Table tennis. Hiking. What's on at the flicks. Sailing or canoeing the disused dredge pits. Prospecting. Golf and rugby league against the other towns. Butterfly collecting. Family time.

The carpenters, who were also employed as miners, like Tom, worked less shifts and more flexible hours than those doing only mine work and were paid a slightly higher rate of 30 pounds a month.

Tom always took his watch off and placed it away from the dusty workbench. He didn't want to count the minutes. He spent a great deal of his time in the work shed off the recreation hall, where usually it was only him and his sometime assistant Una Beel – his 'house boy' – and a few other carpenters during working hours. For Tom, after almost three years on the goldfields, Una Beel had become a friend. Like many locals, Una Beel mixed his time between the goldfields and the native labourers' quarters along the ridge above the European settlement where he lived with his wife and kids, returning less and less to the village of his Buang people down the river as he absorbed the comforts of the white man. Una Beel's set-up was unusual in that of the 1231 labourers only thirty had wives at the native quarters.

Tom had found varying definitions of 'indentured' in a dictionary in the recreation hall's library, and he decided 'apprenticed' was probably the closest description to Una Beel's position in the company town. 'Enslaved' wasn't at all the case. Native labourers were paid 6 pounds a month, no tax, free board in the native labourers' compound and the same forty-four-hour week and six shifts as white miners. That poorly compared with the Europeans 24–28 pounds a month depending on the station of the man on the dredges, no tax, free board, overtime at time and a half and twelve days annual leave on full pay. If white employees worked in wet places they were paid 2 pounds 6 shillings extra per shift. The Native Labour Superintendent, the tall Pom Ted Knight, allotted men into jobs suitable to their strengths, and they were punished the same as the waitman – by docked wages – if they were a no-show, and if any man committed a crime they were imprisoned regardless of race.

There was no favourite duty, but the one job all the men hated was working the myriad underground passages through which water was cannoned to eventually wash the gold. More men had been killed in these subterranean chambers – shot by water cannon, perishing in rock falls, drowning or by other means – than died of natural causes or murders in the township. White and black.

The underground passages were where Una Beel was usually assigned as a labourer. He told Tom that he was aware of the dangers of the pits but that he was all right because he was more cautious than his workmates, especially the ones who had died on the job. He also said that if he or his *wontoks*, his mates, got too frightened or were injured they could leave the job after two years. The money he earned was good and he took some of his wages back to his village, but there it was next to useless. What was highly prized, instead, were the goods he could buy with his money at the BGD Co. store. Bringing knives, matches, blankets and lap-laps – men's traditional wrap skirts, secured with a rope or belt – and especially the steel axes that could replace the stone ones still being used in his place of birth, made him a bit of a hero to his family, as well as increasing his standing in the village.

Most days in the work shed were the best time, for Tom in Bulolo. He was pretty sure it was the same for Una Beel as well, when he saw the look of fascination and excitement come across his friend's face as he used tools on timber that he could only have dreamt of a couple of years earlier. Both men knew that the workshop was a far better place to be than the noisy, stinking grind of eight-hour shifts on the dredges.

Tom was a master carpenter and rookie goldminer when he first arrived in Bulolo. He'd undertaken gold-dredging training the day he got off the plane nearly three years earlier, which meant he could come off the carpentry bench and work many of the jobs that required extracting the gold stuff from the river. His contracted duties, however, mostly included on-site carpentry and joinery, making and maintaining the massive timber sluices connected to the mine that collected the majority of the gold. He also helped either build or maintain all of the substantial European-built houses and native labourers' huts, the halls and offices in the village, and the bridges striding the rivers.

From the pioneering days of gold, when the precious yellow stuff was panned by hand from the rivers and creeks of the Morobe province, timber was as valuable to the miners as the stuff they were prospecting. Mining had well and truly evolved from rudimentary camps of canvas tents to small solid cabins of mostly klinkii and hoop pine sourced from the surrounding rainforest. Timber housed these men. It kept them warm and cooked their food. Gold couldn't do that. Gold was taken out of the river and sent away for company profit. That was the beginning and end of it. It wasn't what made up the town, though it had given birth to it and continued to fund it.

The infrastructure of Bulolo wouldn't exist without the local timber that built the houses, the hospitals, the power station, the dredges they toiled in, the tables and chairs they sat down to eat at. For Tom, it gave a sense of satisfaction. It showed how much his work meant.

For the company, the importance of Tom's carpentry skills was on par with his goldmining, yet that wasn't the case for him. To him, goldmining was toil, an external means to a cold monetary end. In contrast, working the wood with his hands was a spiritual exercise. It gave him an inner sense of happiness and fulfilment that all those years of entrenched religious adherence – up to the moment he renounced his faith – never did.

This wasn't work on the bench in front of Tom. This was what seventy-five years later would be called mindfulness meditation. Breathing and wood and touch. Time didn't exist when he was at one with his tools and timber. The hours it took for the goldmining and village machinations, the carpentry for the company – he always had some leftover for his own projects.

The Dredgemasters, Wally Doe, Arthur Smith and Chester Mayfield, and BDG Co. manager Captain John

Simpson, were decent enough blokes. Mayfield trained up the many Australians who would go up the chain of command on the dredges quicker than any other boss. He had good stories to tell in the Sports Club of working the gold dredges in California and in the Klondike in Canada, and like a few other pioneers who were still around the place, he added to a sense of gold-rush romance that existed at the time.

The miners, a diverse mob of dozens of trades and professions including three doctors – none of them from these high valleys, most of them escaping something or someone – all shared three things: debt and hope and the same gold castle in the air. Just like Tom.

But his was not a nine-to-five bundy on/bundy off job like the miners who worked in groups of three eight-hour shifts to ensure the mine kept churning twenty-four hours a day, three hundred and sixty-three days a year. The only time the metal-on-metal pounding of the dredges stopped was Christmas Day and Good Friday.

It rained nearly every day, or so it seemed to Tom. It was warm throughout the year with some cold nights, and nearly always muggy in his adopted town, 9487 feet above sea level. It was hard to stay dry with the incessant rain, the sweat of the mining work and the work's proximity to the river.

A day or two after a deluge, gold nuggets and dust would often greet the miners, sluicing and tumbling from higher upriver to be gouged from the riverbed by steel digging buckets the size of a sofa and then dumped into smaller buckets on conveyer belts. This continuous line of twenty-two per minute steel digging buckets shunted the valuable gold onto hoppers, which in turn fed a large rotating circular screen that pushed the gold, gravel and sand onto sluiced timber tables to capture most of the gold. If there was a run of the special yellow stuff, it would be all hands on deck.

This was an appropriate nautical phrase, because the dredges – eight in total, each weighing between 1000 and 4000 tons and flown in piece by piece in customised Junkers transport planes from the coast and over the Owen Stanley Ranges to be constructed on site – operated as they floated on the Bulolo, Watut and Markham rivers, churning the riverbeds to depths varying to sixty-five feet. Each dredge was therefore loosely run like any vessel upon the water: hierarchical and with every job on board a specialty. For structures so big they had surprisingly small crews.

The Dredgemaster was the Captain of the ship and head of operations. His ship's bridge served as the dredge's control room, and from here he and the Winchman, the first mate, could see the actual dredging of the alluvial riverbed deliveries being lumped into the buckets and brought into the structures from on high, rather like looking down on operations as they were leaving port on a sea-going vessel.

The Winchman, the overseer, was responsible for the dredge running smoothly. Down the ranks were the stern and bow Oilers, who constantly oiled and greased multiple moving parts; Jig Oilers – much like the able seamen of a ship – who kept the secondary gold-catching jigs working; and a Dayman to undertake running maintenance and repairs.

The dredging operations denuded six to ten acres of jungle every month, so a Shoreman – similar to a wharfie on the docks – with his dozen or so native labourers, would clear the tangled, tropical bush, vine and trees ahead of each dredge, which travelled up to a mile in a year leaving a river-shaped moonscape of tailings on the banks in its wake. Eight dredges. Crews on each one.

Except for the Dredgemaster's role, Tom could do a bit of everything on board the dredge if needed.

Tom was there for a reason. For his family. They were back home in Punchbowl: Mum keeping the house going, kids on Christmas holidays about to go back to school, George starting his second year at high school.

(Another thing to hate his dad for, on top of being so far away for so long, Tom reckoned.) He hadn't seen them for almost three years. Christmases, anniversaries, too many birthdays missed to count. He loved his wife and kids dearly and a day didn't go by when he wouldn't say to himself, or sometimes out loud when alone, 'This is for them ... This is for them.'

In January 1942, there were 119 million cubic yards of alluvial gravel containing 1.3 million ounces of gold and 576,000 ounces of silver extracted from Tom's river town. It was a profitable venture even after the early 1930s gold rush. Then the war entered the picture – and everything stopped.

CHAPTER 3

Unwelcome Visitors

After nearly three years on the goldfields Tom Phelps was a good barometer, and he had come to know Mother Nature as a less-than-benign matriarch. If he could still see a faint outline of Mount Kaindi, it was light rain. Light for New Guinea; equivalent to a downpour for Sydney. If he couldn't see the river a couple of hundred feet away, it was heavy. If he couldn't see the mess hall less than thirty feet away, it was a monsoonal deluge. And he could almost never see the tops of any of the tallest mountains and ridges, as they wore shrouds of cloud as if lassoed around their summits.

Tom wore different clothes when he was mining to when he was woodworking. Mining could be muddy, wet work and if he went from the dredge to the workshop he would have a change of clothes in the locker room of the

Sports Club a couple of hundred feet from the workshop. He also liked to differentiate the two practices so that he would dress for the role, usually white overalls for carpentry, and for the mining work, woollen dungaree pants, long-sleeved shirt always rolled up and heavy work boots, a cap with the visor flipped back on most days and a kerchief around the neck to soak up the sweat.

Tom was in his overalls leaning against the doorframe sipping his tea when he noticed there were only a few high clouds in the bluest of skies, which he knew was unusual. Most days were muggy and overcast and all year not a day went under 20°C or over 30°C (or 86°F and 104°F in Tom's era). The sweat would drip onto his wood if he didn't have a towel handy from the moment he got out of bed. The workshop had been sun drenched all day, illuminating tiny wood particles floating in the air and pinging bright reflections onto various metal surfaces like the steel blades of the circular saw and lathes and the hand tools on wall racks all around the workshop.

At first light the first beads of sweat clung to his skin, whether it was wet or dry season.

Usually at this time of an afternoon Tom would be working on a house in the village or at one of the eight gold-dredging structures that strode the Bulolo riverbanks from the Lower Watut River gorges twenty miles south to the Bulolo River power station, their gold-seeking trunks permanently and constantly submerged and resurfacing, floating in the free-flowing river and doing the prospecting of a few hundred men. These floating ramshackle buildings with long protruding arms appeared out of the river as if someone with too much money slapped a houseboat together without care for aesthetics or the environment.

Bulolo had to be the furthest, least accessible place on earth from everywhere, or at least anywhere Tom could imagine. The war in Europe – for which he was too old and injured to join up, and his son thankfully too young – had been declared shortly before he arrived. He had mates and sons of mates and relatives over there, some for two years and some yet to head off for the battlefields. Even though the Jap attacks on Pearl Harbor were only a month and a half ago, most blokes thought that was still too far away and, anyway, the Japs were attacking America, not an Australian territory's goldfield. What would they want with it? The Aussie militia units, the New Guinea Volunteer Rifles (NGVR), dotted over only a few of the villages in the district, thought so too. The only action they had seen since they were formed at the start of the war was fighting between the local clans, which they let tribal law settle. They were not activated for full-time service until the Japanese invaded the northern coast and they then became the highly effective Kanga Force.

The mindset up on the coast was business as usual. Work the dredges to get that gold just like any other day. Tend the gardens. Make the meals. Care for the patients. Work the wood.

'We'll all be riding out this European war gettin' rich in the yellow sunshine.'

'Nazis'll get lost gettin' here. Anyow, Krauts don't want this place back. O'ready give it back to us.'

'Ities love their food. Only not when they think it's them on the menu. Won't be seein' them 'ere either.'

No goldminer thought two hoots about the Japs. Until they bashed down the back door and invaded the country, that is. Then the old patter was quickly extinguished.

On this day, Wednesday, 21 January 1942, Tom was planing a deckchair arm, apple skin perfectly peeling into circles, the last of an individual section of the whole; the next step would be to join all the cut, chiselled, bevelled and sanded pieces. This was the most pleasurable part of the process for Tom: seeing all the intricately carved jigsaw pieces put squarely in place. A composer hearing their song played by the orchestra for the first time.

The arm of the deckchair was braced in a clamp attached to the workbench he had made from the same klinkii tree as the deckchair. Both were worked by the tools Tom had brought with him from his shed in Punchbowl: the Tital chisels, the two record planers, the plum bob, the long box of Wiltshire files, the Glasster measuring tape, self-built toolbox – most he had engraved with *THP* or *T Phelps* or, if a favourite tool, *Thomas Henry Phelps*.

Tom, now aged forty-five, often thought of the beauty and simplicity of still using the tools from his apprentice days, which had become extensions of his arms as he took the whole of a tree (more like borrowing, he thought), dissecting and manipulating the pieces he formed, making it whole again. And still living. In a workbench, in a deckchair. In the carpentry orders from his co-workers over the past two years on the fields of gold, traded for other goods or paid with cash or an agreed time limit of shouts of beer and cigarettes. For his loves in Punchbowl. A vanity case for Rose. Jewellery boxes for his three daughters, Joy, Shirley and Ann. School pencil case with sliding top for George. He would send them off to travel by two planes (or sometimes one), one ship, three trains and several Sydney Post Master General workers to be delivered to 21 Acacia Avenue, Punchbowl, New South Wales, Australia, 2196.

As he planed, his thoughts turned to home. The kids would be on school holidays right now and giving Rose a version of bedlam. But not Joy, his eldest. Joy was at least equal in the matriarchal stakes with her mother. Ever more so over the years he'd been gone. Tom wondered if George had remembered the back-shed chats of how he was going to be man of the house till he got back and if he was carrying out those duties. He knew George wasn't happy with him being away for so long and so far away, missing so many footy games especially, but hoped by now he understood the situation.

What Tom would never know was the requirement of George to front up to defend family honour in after-school stoushes that would happen on a regular basis at Belmore Oval. It was over his dad getting out of town so soon after the war was declared as if he was running away from fighting in the war like some of the other fathers were at the school. Or it was to defend his sisters if they were picked on in any way and bullied about their father's absence as well. Sometimes the fights were for no reason at all. Stoushes were a regular thing in Punchbowl.

In the earlier stages of these bouts, from age eleven, George rarely came out on top of his adversaries. But his accelerating skills on the rugby league field and take-on-all-comers attitude with his boxing and wrestling at the Punchbowl Police Boys Club meant that by the time he turned fifteen he would be winning the fights. Tom wouldn't read about the fights in the letters he received from home but he did know that they were popular and smart kids and he was proud of his brood.

The work shed was about ten feet from the main dining and recreation hall and was equipped with all the woodworking supplies and tools the carpenters like Tom would need if they didn't have their own tools. It was a comfortable, even inspiring, space for woodworking where he could look through the windows and doorframe at the cloud-enshrined Mount Kaindi, beyond the always-swaying kunai grass and a calmly swirling bend in the river and the town of Wau at the foot of the mountain.

Tom shared his house in Bulolo with two miners, Lofty Burns and David Bone. These past two years had been comfortable, partly due to the accommodation but also because the work was tax-free. When he'd been urged by his mate Jim from McKenzie's timber yard to take up this venture (more like an adventure-venture, he thought at the time), his initial vision was of dirt-floor huts and wild pigs and shitting in holes and going troppo and head hunters and bare-breasted women like he'd seen in the *National Geographic*. It hadn't at all turned out how he'd thought it would.

Tom had read about those men in Ion Idriess's *Gold Dust and Ashes*, a book he reckoned was more a romantic swashbuckling yarn than historical document focusing on Bulolo's gold and its trailblazers in the 1920s and early 30s. More like a movie with Douglas Fairbanks as the Black Pirate who, with his crew of hearty pillaging mates, takes command of a goldmining town in the New Guinea Highlands – though probably better cast with the method actor Errol Flynn. This film would have been a little autobiographical because Flynn actually worked at these mines a few years before, having sailed on a schooner he scammed as his own, made his way to the New Guinea gold rush and created more havoc and sexual digressions than he did in any of his movies.

Tom's ideas were further influenced by the Wild West tales of Cecil Levien, the failed farmer turned Morobe District Officer turned gold-dredging and highland-aviation pioneer, and gold-prospecting pioneers such as William 'Shark Eye' Park, Jim Nettleton and Arthur Darling – men who made fortunes, lost fortunes, forged ties with the natives and brought the Western world, for better or worse, to a place on earth so remote yet inhabited for millennia by hunters and subsistence farmers.

Tom's mind wandered that Wednesday afternoon, taking him back to the thoughts he had before he left Australia. These tales and his mate Jim's reassurances of safety and comfort, along with potentially as much in a week on the goldfields as he could earn in two months or more in Sydney, helped make up his mind. He was sure it wasn't the fortune teller, the local Punchbowl eccentric known as the 'Witch', who, out of the blue, told Tom he was going to go away for a long time. The Witch told him it would be very hard work where he was going and it would be a long walk home. This was a week before Jim McKenzie's offer.

And there was no work in Sydney. It was hand-to-mouth realities even when work did come his way. He was a proud, upstanding man and he had the strongest desire to fill six plates at dinner time. There was no chance Tom would ever be a susso. For Aussie blokes, especially those with a family, this was worse than receiving a white feather in the mail calling you out as a coward, usually for not enlisting. Relying on sustenance coupons meant being humiliated at the special provision stores where your neighbours would see you as a low-life, where you would be mocked by government officials when queueing for unemployment benefits. You could be a susso after two weeks of unemployment, but it was an admission to yourself and everyone that you could no longer support your family and people would cross the street to avoid you.

Tom's mate Jim told him of the Bulolo Sports Club and of all the activities that were part of the Bulolo scene. And the Bulolo brew of choice was mana from heaven/home: cement bags filled with sixteen-ounce cans of Foster's flown in once a week on the big transport planes. Foster's. Melbourne brew. Not KB, Tom's favourite brewed at Kent Brewery on Broadway in Sydney (where his son would become a manager some thirty years later), but good enough, you bet. And coming from home and landing in the hands of blokes with tropical-strength thirsts, it always tasted like it was from God's own brewery.

Tom would come to know the welcoming sound of 'Peter', 'Paul' and 'Pat', the Junkers cargo planes, Guinea Airlines' pack elephants of the sky. The planes that revolutionised aviation and goldmining, and made these remote goldmines the busiest and most productive airfields in the world in the 1930s, got their names from the children's verse:

Two little black birds sitting on the wall
One named Peter, one named Paul
Fly away Peter, fly away Paul
Come back Peter come back Paul.

He never asked how 'Pat' got to be painted on the fuselage of the third plane; he only knew that this plane was acquired after the others.

These transporters were always a pleasant alarm for what was being delivered to and sent out from the people of Bulolo. Moaning, droning, comforting strains that when first heard coming up the valley were like distant rushing whitewater and became a chest-reverberating hum that put a smile on everyone's dial because it meant letters from home, newspapers, crates of beer, cans of film for the flicks, work and recreation supplies. How could he and all his highlander mates not smile? Usually the boxy fat planes brought only good things to and from Wau and Lae and Salamaua and Port Moresby. Tom knew that Bertie was due with some new footballs he would use to train with his first native footy team. And a ton of Foster's. Enough for a week. Happy days.

They'd heard that Lae and Salamaua had been taken by the Japs, and it was only the Port Moresby run that Bertie made now. But all the essential goods were still delivered, because life went on for even the most fearful of the miners.

Every Bulolo resident knew of the encroaching yellow peril even if details and movements of the new enemy were scantily brought to their attention by the few Australian infantry stationed in town. News was scant because these NGVR men simply didn't know what the Japs were up to. The best advice from the authorities given at the increasingly regular town meetings was to carry on as they would do normally – even if the communal belief was that it was only a matter of when, not if, the rising-sun flag would fly over the whole kit and kaboodle.

That day, Bertie Heath and his plane brought something far from joyful.

As Peter approached from a distance, the sound of accompanying little blackbirds was a fluttering, pulsing insistence. Faster, higher-pitched engines. The other aircraft noise Tom could hear definitely wasn't another Junkers, but even if he didn't look at his watch he would still know it was the approximate time for Bertie's arrival.

This was a higher, throatier pitch felt more in the head; a whooshing sound when first heard from below. Then the engine and propeller noise kicked in. Angry wasps, Tom thought.

The unwelcome, higher-octave buzz of an obviously smaller plane meant Bertie was not alone. The buzz changed as it got closer. Alongside Peter's familiar, continuous deep bass frog croak was an underlying chorus of cicadas. It sounded unfriendly, way too low, and more than one.

Tom was still at the door when he witnessed the rare sight of the deepest green of the ridges and the steep denseness of Mount Kaindi in the crisp, clear, sunny afternoon. Beyond the grey waving long grass; beyond the neatly constructed native labourers' huts on the ridge semi-circling the town; beyond the first rise of jungle canopy: three larger, silver birds making a similar flight formation behind the miners' friend, Peter the plane, with Bertie at the helm.

It was a formation that would change many lives forever. Three small planes flying behind Bertie purposely in a one/two triangle formation as if they had suddenly and simultaneously seen Bulolo and zeroed in. Tom knew, even from this distance, that these were planes he had never seen before. He could make out each following plane had fixed wings and small cockpits and he knew enough to know that planes flying that close together would have to be military. As they buzzed closer he saw that two were green and one was silver. The angry wasp pursuers were on Bertie's tail, and why the planes seemed to be tracking no more than a hundred feet above the canopy, Tom couldn't figure out.

Nothing was normal about what he and the gathering men saw. How was Bertie going to land the bulky old freighter given he had no clear aerial view of the runway? There was no chance these buggers were friendly. Was Bertie going to be strafed or was he just being stalked? And for how long? Since his take-off in Port Moresby?

Whatever the answers were, it was clear watching the flying hunters advance up the valley that nothing good was going to come out of this. For Tom Phelps and the Bulolo miners, the Pacific War had arrived.

It didn't take a military genius to know the planes on Bertie's bum weren't cobbers. And Bertie couldn't have given anyone on the ground the answers to any questions even if he did know what was happening, because the transport planes didn't have a two-way radio. There was no communication on board to or from Bulolo or Port Moresby.

Clearly, Bertie could not attempt a landing from the height and angle of his approach; the Junkers was straining like a hippo up a slippery riverbank to get up and over the valley but surely not onto the higher airstrip. It always amazed Tom when he got up close to any of the company's Junkers as to how the hell these metal mammoths got off the ground and stayed in the sky.

Up went Bertie, keeping the same trajectory, the three shiny cheetahs chasing the old hippo. Bertie flew clear of the airstrip and then over the last of Bulolo's houses framed by the clear blue sky. As he reached the level of the highest ridges the Junkers grudgingly turned starboard and lumbered back the way it had come.

The three Japanese Mitsubishi A6M Zeros buzzed almost directly over Tom and Una Beel standing outside the workshop. The sun blasted a reflection from one of the stranger's cockpit glass and made Tom and Una Beel squint and look away simultaneously for a second. Tom knew who they were. The big red circles under the wings told him all he needed to know. Japs.

The Zeros banked a balletic curve in unison the opposite way to Bertie to the northeast then southeast, following the Bulolo River, towards Wau, until they went round the gorge and out of view.

Then came silence, except for the hum of Peter, which was completing a circle of the town, coming back for its probable landing. Much watching of the sky. Japan had come to Bulolo. It knew where they were.

* * *

He was a real bloody character, Jack Hardy. A veteran of the early gold rush, he worked for BGD Co. and lived in a treehouse he built himself in the low hills just off the river bend where the Bulolo becomes the Upper Watut River near the aerodrome. BGD Co. gave Jack the title of Roadmaster – in charge of building and maintaining roads – soon after he arrived, when the gold rush was at its peak, even though he'd never had anything to do with roads back home. He hadn't laid hands on a pick or shovel since then. As Roadmaster he had a never-ending mob of native workers clambering to work with the company because it was considered far and wide by the locals to be the best of the waitman companies for treatment and rewards for their labour.

He was fifty-one, Jack – an old bugger by goldfield standards, ancient by native standards. He had a glass eye, which he took out often to the horror of most of his local crew, some of whom would have to be consoled by fellow villagers upon looking in the hole in Jack's head, which gave him a semi-mythical status.

The number of road labourers varied, and he never counted them anyway; he would simply tell the office how many bois he needed on any week. Whether they were seven or seventy, native males were always 'bois'. The women, not seen very often by the whitefellas and only with their husbands in town, were always Marys.

Roadmasters like Hardo maintained the rough road between Bulolo and the number eight camp near Bulwa. Given there was only one road in and one road out of Bulolo and some small gravel roads in the township, Jack's job wasn't very taxing. Only in the physical sense was Bulolo or little brother mine Bulwa taxing. All work for the company was tax-free, and accommodation was provided. Yet another reason to stay put in the goldfields for the white and native workers alike.

It was all hand tools for the roads, no machinery, and all the grunt work was done by the native labourers. They worked hard when he was around. He was strict yet fair with his bois and knew from experience that if they weren't scrupulously supervised, some of them, still with no sense of Western time and work ethic, would randomly go what the white man called walkabout. Up a jungle path, take a siesta, or wander back to the village. Even if the head native roadworker – the *bos boi*, or *manki boi* – was on the job without Jack there, he could never prevent the workers from doing what was a culturally natural thing to do.

Knowing this Indigenous workforce were a very suspicious mob, with their belief in sorcery, magic, mythical gods, debil-debils and things otherworldly, and that these men of the local Buang clan had only seen whitefellas for the first time ten years earlier, Jack had devised what he thought was a genius way of keeping his bois in line when he wasn't in sight.

Jack enjoyed several tea breaks a day, though his tea was never tea. He would go to his self-made grass lean-to just off in the bush, where he would recline in his deckchair in the shade and listen to opera and jazz and selected crooners on his gramophone. He incrementally sank sometimes two bottles of Scotch with water on his breaks, and often dipped his glass eye into his beverage purely for cleanliness' sake before inserting it back into his eye socket. It hurt like shit and at first he did it to shock and fascinate his bois, but then it became a weird habit, eventually believing the alcohol to be his very own antiseptic solution to things that might enter his eyehole in this disease and bug-filled tropical world.

In the ritual before the breaks, Jack would plunge his pinky finger into the false eye, extract it and point the eyeball at the labourers. Holding it aloft in his hand, eyeball towards them and panning the workers backwards and forwards with authoritarian theatrics, before placing it on a tree stump, he would give variations of:

'Got me eye on you, boys!'

'I'm watching you. Always watching you.'

'Me eye never lies ...'

The bos boi responded, 'Yes, bos, *ai bilong bos lukim yu*, bois.' (The boss's eye is watching you, boys.)

The workers would diligently carry on with their roadwork, knowing Jack's eye on the stump was taking in their every move.

It worked for the first few weeks, until the bos boi had his own stroke of genius. When Jack was out of vision he would put his hat over the all-seeing eye master, which would be the cue for short siestas and general free time until a scout, seeing Jack returning from tea time, would give the call of the bird of paradise – the hat would go back on the bos boi's head, and work would resume.

On the sunny day the Japs flew over, Jack's crew were widening a section of the road at the bend in the river, in sight of the aerodrome. Some Watut bois were below the road crew on a sandbank in the river where the water flowed quickly on either side of them over a few inches of pebbles and sand, washing waitmen's clothes for extra cash or goods. The group washing the clothes were traditional enemies of the road workers, but they hadn't had any battles for some years and both groups liked the waitman's wage too much to fight each other on the job and risk expulsion back to the village.

The two groups looked to the planes almost as one. If it had just been Bertie's familiar droning Junkers, it would have been as if a fly buzzed overhead. These other three, though, were very different in sound. And just as soon as they were spotted they were gone, straight over and banking to the north. Big red spots on the wings. Jack knew.

'They're here. What do they bloody want here?'

'Not friend these ones, bos.'

Bos boi Omas knew who arrived at his home too.

'Jap Jap *painim abus bigpela pisin*.'

'They're huntin' more than birds, Omas,' said Jack as all eyes watched the sky.

There was no fear yet. That only happened when the next lot of planes came over soon after the first three.

For the locals it was hard to feel fear for something with no reference point. An aeroplane was still a waitman apparition, a monster only they knew how to control; to locals, it was a beast to avoid or appease. When the first plane had come ten years earlier, some fled in terror or lay on the ground and wailed in horror, thinking the debil-debils had come to take them. Some placed food beneath the nose of the beast in offering to appease the evil spirit, and when waitmen came from the belly one after another it was as if the beast gave birth.

After almost a decade of waitmen in the Highlands, the villagers had only ever seen good things come from the bellies of the birds. The men who flew them were friendly, bringing the best of the waitman world to the native families.

Whichever man flew these giant birds didn't conjure prejudice. Aussie, Jap, German; it didn't register.

They knew of the waitman enemy, the one coming to take their living places, like they had already down the track in Lau and Salamaua. Which meant they were the natives' enemy also.

Or maybe not for some of them. The more remote people especially, where every waitman was considered at best indifferently, ignored or avoided, at worst to be killed if they posed a threat.

When the second flock of big birds came, the waitman work stopped. Staying alive and being with your own took priority over anything to do with the white man and his village. Every native to a man fled.

CHAPTER 4

Zero Return

They came from the same direction as their first flyover. This time, though, reports state the three fighters were joined by two more Zeros and two Aichi D3A bombers launched from the Nippon aircraft carrier *Shokaku*. The same higher-octave buzz as before. A chorus of cicadas joined by duelling bass notes. More than the last lot, making it sound even less friendly than the first visit. This time the noise of Bertie's plane was replaced by the town's air-raid siren, set off by Buster Mills, the laidback and effective NGVR sentry on duty at the time. Bulolo had all new sounds. Eerie and ominous. From friend and foe.

The very sound that defined the town – the twenty-four-hour steel clanking of all eight dredges – ceased completely for the first time on a work day since Dredge 1 cranked up eleven years before, shut down when the news of a swarm of enemy aircraft heading their way from Madang in the northwest was transmitted.

The decision to flee was more or less the universal option for Jack's roadworker bois and those below them washing clothes in the riverbed. After the first flyover, Jack had told them that they were the enemy and wanted to steal their homes and kill them all, white men and black. They bolted, all of them, the instant they saw the ensemble of planes fly over. They sensed what a hunting party going in for the kill looked like. The first big birds were the hunters' scouts spotting their prey. Word got round instantly to locals, that if the silver birds and more came back, then it was best to get away from that fight. To a man they headed upstream, downstream, into paths, anywhere away from the waitman town and the *bigpela pisin bilong* Jap, the big birds of the Jap.

Jack Hardy stood alone on the road bend above the river. He knew that no glass-eye trickery was going to get these bois back.

'Friggin' hell, do I run with them, what do I do?'

Jack had chosen over the years to have only brief contact with his fellow Aussies in town; he liked it that way in his self-built jungle lair. Bumping into them getting supplies once every couple of weeks was enough for him. And for them. He spent more time in the scattered Buang settlements. Some of the elders and the folks in the village thought Jack was a good man because he helped recruit the young boys for waitman work, but some other elders weren't so happy about that. They thought all their young men exiting the village and increasingly staying away meant ceremonies and traditions were being lost.

Suddenly by himself as he watched his fleeing workers, Jack thought it might be a good time to get reacquainted with his countrymen again.

The Junkers approached the airstrip as the Jap planes headed up the valley, squashing the distance between Bertie's tail and themselves.

Six bounces on the portside wheel, one or two on the starboard and lots of wobble, but Bertie had landed. It was never a smooth landing in Paul or Peter or the newest transporter, Pat. Or any plane landing at Bulolo, for that matter. The airstrip was cleared grassland, maintained by hand, yet this was land you could never quite contain and maintain for a smooth touchdown.

In town, all were unnerved by the wail of the unfamiliar air-raid siren. Those who were watching Bertie's landing and the incoming strangers, men coming out of buildings, up tracks from the bush and up the riverbank, all felt the heightened sense of danger that had built steadily from the first Jap visit. Those within earshot of Captain John Simpson, BGD Co. manager, took the shouted advice to find shelter in the bush, shelter anywhere but the town's structures. There were no NGVR officers, commissioned or otherwise, to be seen, which Tom thought strange. He hadn't spotted any Rifles since the first Jap planes flew over and entered their world.

Tom, like other townsfolk and miners from the nearest dredge to town, stood transfixed and made rapid, on the spot, individual decisions.

'Japs are back! They got bombers with them!' shouted young Jim Huxley coming off his eight-hour shift as a newly arrived oil jigger and trotting past Tom.

Tom replied, 'Where's your old man?' Jim's father Richard, known as Dahlia Dick, was another carpenter on the goldfields who had worked alongside Tom a lot of the time and who got his nickname because of the meticulous care he took of his flower beds.

'Dunno. Should get under cover somewhere, eh,' young Jim said, pausing for a moment to talk with Tom.

'Go find him and the Brass and see what's next,' Tom said. Jim started off again as Sergeant Van Vandenburg, who never answered to his birth name Richard, appeared suddenly on the move with Jim.

'No time for that, mate – get cover away from the buildings. Come on, they're gonna hit. Into the gun pit – main store trench, go, follow us!'

The machine-gunning from two Zeros started as Bertie Heath and his young flying mate and apprentice Malcolm Goad jumped from the plane's cargo hatch. Unaware of their angry flying companions' return with reinforcements and the imminent attack until the bullets started tearing up the grass airstrip, they ran like buggery in a direct line to the slit trench beside the BGD Co. main store at the side of the aerodrome.

As they slid into the trench Bertie almost piled onto Reg Gillingwater, who caught Bertie at the bottom of the trench like a garbo had thrown him a sack of spuds.

Bertie turned back to Peter as the first bullets hit. Two more subsequent attack planes had arrived to back up the first, and together they strafed the dying mammoth. Within a minute it was in flames.

Reg was still holding Bertie when he reassured him, 'You and the young fella orright? Lucky stars. Youse made it, mate.'

Bertie let him know the bad news first. 'Bloody beer didn't.'

'Little bastards,' Reg replied.

The first of the bombs hit the main storage building. Seconds later an ear-splitting explosion had men diving to the ground or rushing the next man into the gun pit, anywhere low and flat. Of course the Japs hit the fuel depot, the orange and red and black mushroom cloud's heat felt on the faces of the men in the pit.

Buster Mills was in the trench too. He was on sentry duty at the airstrip when the first shit hit the fan. It was Reg Gillingwater who took the random radio telephone call in the main store that altered the township: the warning that Jap planes were heading from Madang in the north directly towards them. It was Buster who set off the air-raid alarms. Lucky for everyone in town that they were in the know, because other towns hadn't got the message. If not for the warning, many would have been machine-gunned or blown up in the targeted buildings or dredges they were recently standing in.

Planes Paul and Pat, sitting like stationary carnival ducks at the end of the airstrip, were strafed almost simultaneously by the three other Zeros, one after the other with repeated flyovers; they were completely destroyed after a third pass. Slaughtered immolated elephants.

The Japs had done their homework. They knew what to hit and when.

The bombers were as clinical as the fighters, coordinating their runs with the Zeros, turning Bulolo buildings into burning splinters.

The power station: gone. Anything that looked like a main building: gone. The mess hall, which included the cinema and kitchen, machine shops, library and theatre: destroyed. The communications tower and telegraph poles: all taken out, bombed and strafed and mostly on fire. All in all an impressive fifteen minutes of precision airmanship and pinpoint accuracy. The destruction was noted with awe by the men – none of them soldiers – who were scared stiff, frozen in fear and wouldn't have known what precision airmanship was before that moment. All, however, knew they were in the middle of the biggest shit fight they hoped they would ever see. They were no longer goldminers. From the first bullet that tore into their town, they became casualties of war.

The Japs no doubt hit the planes first because they knew they were the only means of escape for the populace. There was no way the Junkers planes would be anything but useless in defence, but as insurance, the fuel depot's devastation was confirmation that this small town would never take part in this war.

Not one of the eight dredges were touched. The extraction of gold and its product were of no interest to Japan or its war effort. That's why, in the post-mortem analysis by all in Bulolo, this was such a surprise attack. Why our mining town? Coastal towns were traditional targets for the part they could play in the movement of supplies and troops, but what strategic factor was behind taking out this place? The planning of the evacuations to come, especially the quandary of where the bloody hell to evacuate to, would make these questions even harder to answer.

Tom had done what Van Vandenburg had told him: he'd run, with a dozen others, to the only armed weapon pit, the one with a WWI Vickers anti-aircraft gun, the only anti-aircraft defence in town, which was in place on a tripod swivel mount to hit attacking planes in all directions. It had last been used for training drills five years previously. He reached the pit that Bertie was in before turning to see if Una Beel had followed him. He saw only white goldminers running God knew where, diving into other pits or up tracks, attempting to escape the Japanese lottery.

Tom had a clear view of his path to the pit from his workshop. It was just one bomb. He didn't cover his ears or close his eyes; he needed to see.

It didn't just take out the wood and metal workshop and adjoining buildings. It ended everything he knew up here, everything he had created.

Buster Mills had managed to load the WWI vintage gun with a WWI canvas-wrapped vintage cartridge with surprising speed. Until that point it had been assumed that no one except the NGVR boys knew how to use it, but Buster put paid to that notion. Tom had always thought the gun was possibly a memorial to those lost in 1914–1918. Or a training piece, never expected to be needed in a real, live situation.

Neither Bulolo nor its environs had ever seen military action in its 60,000-year human history. The only battles in these parts – and they were centuries-old, frequent and just as brutal and lethal as any mechanised European warfare – were hand-to-hand with the aid of bows and arrows, spears, machetes and sorcery.

The noise of the old Vickers ... *fut-fut-fut-fut-fut-fut* ... paused only when the operator took his hand off the large central fire button between the hand grips ... *fut-fut-fut-fut-fut-fut* ... was aimed at the Jap planes, and was bloody deafening and never reassuring. This time Tom did put his hands up to cover his ears.

The old ammo ran out after five Zero and bomber flyovers. The violence of the ear-splitting gunfire did not translate to any enemy damage even as they passed over close enough to spit on the arse of the bastard yellow bellies. Tom checked and saw no noticeable hits to the

Emperor's flying force and, even if they'd made a hit, they wouldn't have made an impact from this Jurassic defence machine.

The Vickers gun had been built to shoot down biplanes in World War I in the first-ever battles that involved aircraft: German bombers dangled the bombs by their hand as they steered the plane to the target and then let the bomb go on their target by sight. In 1942, Zeros were the Ferraris of fighting planes; the fastest and most lethal in the world. The Aussies' Vickers gun was next to useless. It was like attempting to shoot down a peregrine falcon in full flight with an air rifle. Bulolo residents didn't know that before the firing started, but they did once it had stopped.

The men in the pit were yapping over each other, shouting about what they saw as an obvious pattern of bombing and strafing the crap out of the main structures, debating if they should run for better cover and arguing about how long before the Japs got out of there to refuel. The main question was if it was a better idea to just wait it out where they were, or run. The answer came when a single Zero made another run towards the main store, towards the pit, towards the men, strafing in a different line yet with the same meticulous aim. Sergeant Van Vandenburg had taken up position in front of the pit so as to best see the Jap movements, and he saw the line of fire streaming towards him. He only got out the first 'Get down!' when he was hit on the side of the head and crumpled between Tom and a bloke Tom couldn't remember ever meeting. When he hit the deck he screamed, 'I've been hit, boys! Carry on without me!'

Reg Gillingwater was sitting crossed-legged with a clump of turf in his crotch at the back of the pit. He held the turf aloft. 'Saw it bounce off ya melon, Sarge. Ya got no blood, but shit, how close was that? Japs doing a bit of gardening, eh.'

Van Vandenburg sprang to his feet, felt his head and then took command immediately at his most vocal. 'No, I haven't been bloody well hit, boys – carry on, give it to the little bastards!'

The attack was over in fifteen minutes, but those minutes changed a town and men's lives forever.

CHAPTER 5

Fate Sealed

PUNCHBOWL, 1938. George Phelps had his first paying job. He was nine years old. He and Keithy Jones were proud to be scooter couriers for George's dad, Tom. George had a list of materials to buy at the Punchbowl Hardware on the Boulevarde and then he was to deliver over dozens of footpaths to a house five miles over the tracks in Greenacre where his dad was working. Tom was waiting for George to bring him a sack of red ochre, the icing on the cake of the job he was finishing off, a solo effort replacing rotted pine decking and rafters. No one in town could have done better. It had been a long time since even a small job like this had come along and he was determined to do it well. He had come in under budget and even had a few rafters to spare, which he could return to the timber yard and reimburse the impressed owner.

Tom had ten poles in place in the ground, lined along the deck to form the railing. All he needed to do was to cement them in. Tom had told George that red ochre was the most essential material on the job because it was the best holding agent when mixed with the cement before pouring. He wanted George to believe he was an important part of the job. He wanted his son to feel valued.

It did make George feel an even greater sense of obligation, and he pushed the scooter with extra gusto with every plant of his foot on the footpath. Keith held his mate's sides ever tighter, one foot on the scooter board, the other across the top of the box of ochre, pushing down tightly so it wouldn't bounce out.

Earning pocket money for his first job with Dad was bonzer, and George would split it with Keithy. It was only fair too, because the scooter that George was doubling Keith on was, in a way, a hand-me-down from Keith in the first place. Keith's old man worked at the tax office and was the only dad with a proper full-time job. Everyone knew that George and Johnny and Ron got Christmas presents from Santa that were actually Keith's past Christmas and birthday gifts. It was quietly and subtly done. They were usually patched up nicely by one of the dads to look like new: a coat of paint to make the police car look like it was from a different country, some tassels added to the handle bar, a different colour sail for the toy yacht. Nothing was ever said about it. Just about every family they knew was cash-strapped. Sometimes one of the boys got a present that was a fifth-down-the-line reworking of the original, but someone always made sure it all worked fine, sometimes better than the second time round.

George did his research with Keith, had tracked the Greenacre address – 17 Chiswick Road – in the *Gregory's Street Directory* that was kept in the nook of the phone stand at his house, and Keith had hold of the hand-drawn mud map the whole way. They had drawn it up together. Whenever he needed to look at it he gripped tighter with one arm around George's waist and held it out to spout the necessary instructions. He didn't make any mistakes as he played navigator, shouting turns and directions at just the right time for George to brake or steer at the crucial time.

He turned off Waterloo Road and Keith let out a whoop, 'This is it, this is it!'

'Where. Here?'

'Nah, up on the right a bit. This is the street!'

Even numbers on the left, odd numbers on the right, the opposite going back the way they came.

'Seven! That means five houses up on the right!' called Keith the navigator.

'There's my dad's truck!'

They were scooter legends.

Tom was at the back of the tray of the truck parked right outside the house he was working on. He clapped them in down the footpath.

'There they are! Quicker than any truck delivery. Good on ya, boys.'

George put his foot on the heel brake and stopped on the grass verge next to the truck tray. He was beaming up with achievement at his dad.

'G'day, Mr Phelps.' Keith hopped off the scooter.

Tom looked at the back of the scooter and then his eyes tilted up, following a neat, thin line of red running along the footpath. He put his arm round his son's shoulder.

'Keithy boy, how are ya, mate?'

'Yeah, good, sir. We made this.' Keith held out the map.

'Said I'd give you both a lift back home, right?' Tom said.

'Yeah, we know. We can wait till ya finished,' said George.

'Pretty much finished now, mate. You know if you wanna retrace your steps to anywhere, all ya gotta do is follow your beaut map back the way you came. Turn it upside down and Bob's your uncle.' Tom thought he'd play with them a bit.

'Whaddya mean, Dad?'

Tom pointed from the box tied to the scooter to the red line up the footpath, made brighter by the sun belting on the glary, white cement.

'Arr jeez ...' George and Keith said in unison.

The red ochre had almost finished its last spill as Tom took the sack from the box on the scooter. 'Maybe I should call you Hansel and Gretel. Those bright bloody breadcrumbs were always gonna get you back home. At least back to the hardware, anyway.'

'Arr Dad, I'm ... Oh God, sorry, Dad.'

'It's all right, mate. Reckon the next rain, we're going to have a lovely pink pathway from here to Punchbowl Hardware, aren't we, eh?'

'Sorry, Mr Phelps, thought I had my foot on it,' Keith said.

'Don't worry about it, mate. You blokes come and help me clear up. Gotta put some rafters on the truck. Sweep up some shavings. Tools back in the box.'

'I can scrape up the red ochre, Dad. Put it back in one of your sacks.'

'Don't be silly, mate; be pretty bloody funny, though, wouldn't it, eh? Nah, help your old man, come on. Bloody funny. Gonna have to follow it back in the truck, though, aren't we, eh? See Hansel and Gretel's track winding back to good ol' Punchbowl.'

Tom had placed the rafters on the roof with his own system of ladders and winches and ropes for the heavy stuff. He often worked with other carpenters and builders and alongside other tradesmen, but he liked working on his own mostly, his only assistants his truck and his tools and sometimes his son.

With the last of the rafters he had looped a rope on the end to make it easy to pull down on the ground from the roof and then slide it to the truck. He triple-knotted the other end for a good hand grip and left it dangling for easy access when he left the day's work.

George and Keith followed Tom to the house's deck.

'Stay back a bit, boys. I'll bring the thing down, then you can both help me lift 'em to the truck. You staying for dinner, Keithy?'

'Dunno, Mr P.'

Tom hit the last step up onto the deck as the rope knot caught in his overall's shoulder buckle. It pushed the rafter forward and too far over the other side of the roof, and it swung back and inwards, too quickly for Tom to duck or weave. The end of the rafter came squarely at his shin, smashing the bone and sliding to his ankle, opening a gouge from shin to foot and making a hole to his heel, breaking the navicular bone on top of his foot, blood immediately flowing out over his trouser leg. It forced

Tom backwards and through a square frame of the railing he had put in place the day before.

George went to his dad as quickly as he could, and Keith moved to stop the swinging rafter so it couldn't do any more damage.

His dad didn't really make much noise in the horrible bleeding catastrophe. Tom sat up, then stood up almost straightaway and walked towards his truck with what George thought must have been superhuman powers but what was just Dad being the always laconic, she'll be right, get on with it dad. How could he talk so calmly and not be screaming in pain?

Tom talked as he walked. 'I'll be right, mate. I'll wrap this up for now and stop the bleeding. Throw your scooter in the back and jump in, boys. I'll collect my stuff tomorrow.'

George was dumbstruck. 'Dad, you can't drive. I'll get an ambulance. I'll call on the telephone from inside.'

'Nah, mate, the missus in the house is a night nurse. She'd be asleep. You can work the clutch on the truck. Think you can do that?'

George looked to Keith with an *Oh shit!* expression. 'Of course, Dad.'

Tom ripped open his trouser leg and grabbed an old towel from his rag bucket in the back of the truck.

'We'll get on home to the best healer in town,' he said as he started to wrap his wound. 'Your mum and her magic black ointment. Better than any quack on earth.'

* * *

BULOLO, 1942. The bandage Tom had wrapped around his foot and up to his shin was more often on than off. More often wet than dry. The old wound from the work injury in Sydney had opened up and a patch of tropical ulcers kept residence on the reopened scar. 'My very own horrible bloody volcanoes,' Tom would call them. The little volcanoes with the purple rims looked like a rat had gnawed holes and left red lumpy balls in the crater above a pus-yellow base, the surrounding skin charred and blackened as if fixed on by a blow torch.

That's what Doc Eric Giblin stared down at, and through a grimace made Tom feel less than confident about his enlistment prospects. He wanted to do his bit and add to the minuscule military defence the Australians were forming to fight against who knows how many thousands of invaders they felt were rapidly surrounding them. If the bastards could launch bombers way out at sea and blow this far-flung town away for no bloody reason, then who was to say what could happen next.

The order had been given by the War Cabinet in Canberra, and the commanding officer of the NGVR, Major Bill Edwards, was tasked with recruiting all white British men (which Australians were classed as) between the ages of eighteen and fifty for immediate military service.

For days after the attack, most men still under the heavy shock and trauma of bombardment, the main activities seemed to be wandering aimlessly around the smouldering town or checking out the damage. Men not much older than eighteen and not many over twenty-two who were part-time militia became full-time soldiers. Whole crews of gold dredgers – all the men of Dredges 1, 5 and 7 – signed up, kitted up and had marching orders for immediate deployment eighty-five miles on the hoof to Lae for action that was already taking place.

That's what Tom wanted: to fight the bastards. Answers to the questions of his physical ability and age were contained within the doctor's grimace. He knew with that look what the outcome would be.

'This was going to be amputated at one stage? Medically recommended. You told me that story,' was the doctor's opener.

'Yes but my wife fixed me up – got me back on my feet, literally. Told you that one too,' Tom reminded him.

'Ah, the magic black ointment. Yes, well God bless her.'

He knew he was fit enough. 'I do full shifts on the dredge, train up the local boys. Play the full eighty minutes. Admittedly it's touch footy. Still.'

Giblin looked over his glasses. 'Given they have a stench about them, Tom, and they are quite deep, it tells me they're advanced in their infection. That and the malaria. Nothing will improve or help the cause tramping through this country kitted up and carrying a weapon.'

There was another doctor with Giblin. Noel McKenna was the government medical officer at Wau, but since the Jap attack, like so many in New Guinea, his station had changed overnight: he was now the Commanding Officer of NGVR Medical Detail and newly appointed temporary enlistment officer. And, along with his fellow medic, Giblin, he was the fate-sealer for Tom and 200 other men.

'Mate, I'd love ya to join us. Bloody happy for ya to grab a weapon and wipe out a few of the little buggers with us. The more the merrier. But you know ...'

'You got blokes ten years older than me going in. Bloody Alf Staunten's fifty bloody seven.'

'Already in the Rifles. Those older blokes were doing weekend training since the bloody big show began, mate. He was at Gallipoli.'

'No one's got combat experience in that bloody terrain. When have Aussies fought jungle bloody battles?'

'Well, you're right there,' said McKenna.

'It's a level playing field, right?' Tom said.

Giblin quipped, 'Not quite so level for some, Tom. Get home to family, they're the priority.'

McKenna agreed. 'Look, there's no dishonour in going back to defend your family, mate. Scuttlebutt is that Darwin is not going to be the only Australian city to feel the samurai sword.'

Tom knew he'd exhausted his line of imploring to stay on.

That was it, then. Fate sealed. Gold-dredge workers who lived in Bulolo for a very specific purpose became either full-time soldiers or unemployed evacuees. Either way, those who had enlisted and those who were to be evacuated shared one thing – they knew nothing of what lay ahead. Either way, they knew it was not going to be a party.

The whole process of selection was random. Some older Volunteer Rifles wouldn't be fighting and stayed on to be cooks or civvies away from any frontline, helping out the war effort in any way they could. For some it wasn't compulsory to enlist or evacuate. Tom knew of a few miners-turned-soldiers he could run or swim rings around on the football field or in the pool. How he was deemed unfit and others were signed up without having a physical went beyond any logic he could fathom. There was nothing left for Tom to do. Bulolo could no longer operate as a mining or even civilian town; the bombings had put paid to that. And the threat hung heavily. It was day one as headquarters for the NGVR and newly formed ad hoc commando unit Kanga Force, sent in to fortify the part-timers. An army barracks was hastily prepared for military action, while a plan was prepared to evacuate all non-military British inhabitants.

Tom felt better knowing a few blokes who'd made it onto the Wau evacuation list with him. His housemates, Lofty Burns and David Bone, as well as his neighbour Max Howard, would share the trip in his group, the first scheduled to hit the trail to Wau. The plan, after flying out of Wau, was getting to Port Moresby and shipping their souls to the home soil of Cairns in North Queensland. They would then catch a train home before the end of footy season, if it hadn't been cancelled. It was a simple enough plan, but even simple plans have obstacles. They were as happy as Tom was that if anything got out of shape, and it was as good as an odds-on bet on Phar Lap that it would, they had each other's backs. That was comforting. Not much else was.

The white, male, 'British', 'unfit for service', elderly miners – who to a man could grind out an eight-hour manual-labour shift day in day out – would leave Bulolo in staggered groups of fifteen to twenty men and roughly the same number of carrier bois – the ones who hadn't disappeared when the bombs fell – who used to work as labourers and house boys. Tom's mate Una Beel was right by him.

All in all, 200 odds and sods who failed the enlistment cut were theoretically destined to get a step closer to wives and families, or get even further away from wives and families, than they already were.

It was an unspoken pact that a miner would never ask another miner about his family; a man had to initiate a conversation about his loved ones. Their eccentric choice of occupation meant any number of family situations sent them to their remotest places of work. Those couple of dozen blokes with wives and children who had lived in Bulolo with their families had evacuated the women and children before Christmas. They had stayed on like the rest of the miners still employed by BGD Co. even after the town was made useless for mining or any other business. All of them were white and male, and not one was able-bodied. Most of the others had enlisted, some were on the march. When Tom glanced around at the men marshalled for the hike, he wasn't sure whether some of the blokes would even make it upriver to Wau. For many

Bulolo blokes, life was the same every day: wake up, oil that jig for eight hours, sink a few gallons of beer until they passed out. And repeat. On days off they'd just cancel the eight hours' oiling.

The plan was to hike it to Wau and then fly out. There was no choice. Well, there was but it came with no protection from the Australian Imperial Force, which would be fighting in a jungle theatre and quite possibly defending their ruined town as the Japanese hordes parachuted in. If you stayed, you would not be captured. As a civilian you would not become a prisoner of war. The Japs made those choices, and the Kanga Force boys told the miners they'd be dead before they could call for dear old Mum. Most wouldn't be armed, so more than likely they would run you through with a bayonet or take off your head with a knife or samurai sword.

The Wau Mining Company's planes were the ticket out of any of that, and even without taking a vote it was unanimous to follow that plan.

* * *

The last men they ever saw in Bulolo were a bloke they called Saksak the Jap and two miners who were now enlisted soldiers carrying rifles instead of spanners. Saksak had run the small trade store, and Tom thought he was Malaysian or Indonesian. Before the bombing calling him a Jap wasn't such an insult.

Tom and his old civi troop needed to gear up for the nineteen-mile jaunt to Wau, and so they went to the store to top up their packs before giving them over to the native bois to carry. The front of the store was no more, and the area around it still smouldered, smelling of bomb and burn. The storeroom at the back had survived the carnage, and this was where they got packets of raisins and hunks of cheese and oranges that only had a few days left in them, rolly papers, billy tins, and extra tobacco tins, a few more tins of meat and some knives and implements for the overnight trek.

There was a caged area at the very rear where some of the all-important beer supplies were usually held along with stationery and laundry items that would never again be up for sale. Everything left in town, down to the last tin of beef, was to be utilised by the army.

Besides the pilot Bertie Heath and apprentice Malcolm Goad, the beer was the only thing that made it out of the wreckage of Bertie's plane. When the fires on the plane subsided some of the troops discovered that only the top layer of beer had exploded. Most of the three tons of Foster's had survived. Most of that was consumed on the night of the bombing, to counter the heavy shock that lingered for days, and also as an act of defiance to the Japs, who hadn't completed their task of destruction.

Tom and his friends came upon Saksak locked up inside the cage, sitting on a box looking through the steel squares at the men he knew well, gazing through thick horn-rimmed spectacles at each man he made eye contact with.

Whenever any of the miners queried the guards as to what the bloody hell Saksak was doing in the kalabus or approached him with apologies or reassurances, Saksak would deliver his mantra: 'She be light, mate. She be light, mate.' Always with that smile of his like he was just waiting on word from the Brass that it was all a mistake and he would join up with one of the other groups and see you down the track. As if he wasn't really going to be taken to Australia and interred in a prisoner of war camp in country New South Wales and eventually take part in a mass breakout before being shot and killed by an Australian guard performing the same duties as those guarding him on the other side of the cage. Eight guards, two at a time in shifts of two-hours-on-six-hours-off, watched over the inconspicuous middle-aged shopkeeper everyone was friendly with.

One of the guards on duty as the first of the miners

milled about was young Jim Huxley, last seen by Tom as a middle oiler on Dredge 8, now Private Jim Huxley attached to the medical unit. He said to no one in particular, 'Yeah it's over the bloody top. So's Tuckey. He's gone from Winchman to führer overnight. Got eight of us keeping watch on the bastard. This here's us following orders from someone we sank schooners with. Smashin' a cooked pea with a Sherman tank.'

Kel Austin piped up. 'Ol' Sakky the sago wouldn't hurt a fly.'

'Neither would probably all the other Jap workers all over this bloody island,' said the other guard, Buster Mills.

'Heard there's plans of a round-up of the German missionaries and the Itie miners too. All enemies now, mate, military fatigues or not.'

'The Bulawat mob? There's only Italians up there running that mine,' said John Lovett, the Dayman on 6 and 8.

'No one from anywhere's going to be mining now, mate,' said Wally Head. 'Don't matter where ya from.'

Buster shared more. 'Word is they're getting a free ride back to Sydney and they've got camps for each nationality in the bush.'

Tom looked at young Jim's shirt and was curious. 'The Red Cross armband?'

'You got it, right? What the bloody hell. Reckon there was eight of us in the room and Tuckey just pointed and said, "Cage the Jap, all a ya."'

'She be light, mate. She be light, mate,' Saksak the Jap said. But nothing would be right for a long time.

CHAPTER 6

Scorched Earth

Jesus Christ Almighty, were the Aussies working in cahoots with the Japs or what? They had hit Bulolo hard, the Japs, in a perfect fifteen-minute storm of phenomenal airmanship – all planes, all communication towers and power supplies and most main buildings, gutted write-offs. The recreation centre, for Christsakes. Then they heard that their own boys were going to make a five-fold bloody job of it. None of the men on the march could fathom it when they got the rumour second-hand, but that's how it was since the Jap visit. As soon as they stopped being miners they were given hand-me-down news or directives from the Brass they never saw. Nothing was ever direct. On the dredges, there were no Chinese whispers. News came from the source with no bullshit attached. A lot of the time this had to do with the safe running of the steel-and-timber mammoths. One bit of false information could mean the loss of a limb or worse and was the main reason the native bois were kept away from the internal machinery. It was difficult to translate and educate the dangers of working the monsters.

It turned out the rumours were true. The higher-ups had promoted Major Norman Fleay to Lieutenant-Colonel and his first order was the demolition of Bulolo and its little brother mining town Bulwa, in case of imminent Japanese troop landings. A scorched-earth policy was his to implement. Bill Edwards, still head honcho of NGVR, was ordered to work in conjunction with the newly formed Kanga Force and take orders from twenty-five-year-old Fleay, a man in turn twenty-five years younger than Edwards. Kanga Force would go on to be very effective jungle commandos and, alongside the native bois, vital in knowing enemy positions in the months ahead.

Fleay ordered his Staff Captain Cameron West to lead the destruction of the town with the Kangas when his word came down. It only took a couple of days for Captain West to earn his nickname, Snifter. Even the gathering miners were onto it and could see how his moniker was richly deserved because he was never far away from Fleay's backside.

The last bit of information Fleay got from anyone in a position to know anything was that the Japs would be dumping airborne troops to be a ground force whenever the heavy cloud lifted. A bloody lot of airborne troops. He was warned not to be late in carrying out demolitions. The Japs had ensured with their pinpoint accuracy that Bulolo had lost radio contact with forward observation posts, so the final call had to come from Fleay. He made the intuitive move swiftly. All hands were now in military defence mode, and the miners – in ten groups of roughly twenty apiece – were either on the hoof or preparing for the staggered start of their slog to the airlift. Kanga Force and NGVR were determined to leave bugger-all for the evil Japanese, and miners with their carriers were told to get out of town and head up to Wau.

The damage would be done mainly with dynamite and petrol. Detonators were wired up to all three power stations, and the same for the complete destruction of the three bridges over the Bulolo River, BGD Co.'s refrigeration plant and its oil derricks, along with the European hospital (but not the native hospital, possibly because it was too ill-equipped to be of any use to the Japanese). No stores were to be left standing. All houses and infrastructure, every stick the company had built was to be doused in petrol and set alight. Anything edible was to be destroyed, even the fruit and vegetables growing in patches across the town. The roads and airstrip were to be dug up and turned into craters, useless for landing aircraft. Any weaponry and ammunition that a soldier couldn't carry out was to be put on the pile that would be topped with a couple of sticks of dynamite, to the last gun.

The only man-made structures to escape annihilation were to be the pulses that pumped the blood of Bulolo. The dredges were to be dismantled and rendered inoperable and vital parts disabled and hidden so the little bastards couldn't operate the company's monoliths and get their hands on the river's gold.

The boss of BGD Co., John Simpson, complained to representatives of the Australian government that it was going a wee bit over the top to destroy what was in reality his company's town. Anything and everything standing in the place was the property of BGD Co. He knew he'd lost all his employees and therefore his hugely profitable business. Next would be all his property. But this was war. Kanga Force and the Australian Imperial Force through the Australian government were boss. And they were going to destroy it all.

The first house was set alight as Tom's party hit the road. Tom's group of nineteen were almost opposite as they saw Snifter slopping a bucketful of petrol on the foundations all round one of the family homes. It was Sam Weeks's place, Tom thought, a three-bedder. Taking no time to chuck a match on his work, Snifter stood back, watching the flames reach over the roof in under a minute. About twenty of his men, equipped with the same incendiary equipment, were scattered over the lawns and up the roads of the town, carrying out their destructive work.

Tom didn't think it was one of his group's houses, but that didn't matter. It was all their homes. They were all going to lose. The feeling of dread and ending and loss put a lump in all their throats.

'Don't watch, fellas!' was the shout from Canadian Lance Donovan as they walked up the gravel road towards Wau.

Ollie Phelan up front turned and consoled his new hiking mates. 'Little fuckers won't take our houses or heads, boys. All for a good cause.'

By God, Tom wished he could get or send news to and from home. He knew the other men wished that too. But there was no chance. Deadly accurate Japanese pilots destroyed the Bulolo thread of communication. The NGVR boys didn't have emergency back-up comms and were improvising just like the miners were. The hope was that Wau was still a functioning town and would give them a way to get in touch with their loved ones.

When he saw the flames licking the first house, the designated family three-bedder of similar size to his

Punchbowl pile, Tom thought of the kids and Rose and what they would be feeling about him so far away. They must have seen newsreels or heard the news on the radio about the Japanese incursions, if that was what they were calling it. They must have, like Tom, thought that the Japanese had them surrounded. He reckoned George would probably think he had been taken prisoner or been killed.

* * *

Tom was among the first nineteen whitefellas and the fifteen carriers who struck out together at the point of evacuation from Bulolo to Wau. They were:

Kelvin Austin. Council worker. Dayman, Dredge 6, 8.

David Bone. Motor mechanic. All duties, Dredge 2, 3, 4.

Lofty Burns. Bricklayer. Middle oiler, Dredge 2.

Len Cohen. Lawyer. All duties, Dredge 8.

Lance Donovan. (Canada.) Goldminer. All duties, Dredge 3.

Eric Giblin. Medical doctor.

Jim Hargreaves. (United States.) Original occupation unknown. All duties, Dredge 6, 8.

Wally Head. Farmer. Shoreman, Dredge 1, 2, 3, 4, 5, 6, 7, 8.

Jack Hill. Original occupation unknown. Middle jig oiler, Dredge 2.

Max Howard. Bank teller. All duties, Dredge 2, 3, 4.

John Lovett. Boilermaker. Dayman, Dredge 6, 8.

Will Marshall. Engineer. All duties, Dredge 2, 3, 4.

Ernie O'Hara. Butcher. Dayman, Dredges 2, 3, 4.

Ollie Phelan. Truck driver/mechanic. Dredge duties.

Tom Phelps. Carpenter. Dayman. All duties, Dredge 2, 3, 4.

Colin Phillips. Plumber. Bow and stern oiler, Dredge 6.

Leonard Schrater. (German.) Original occupation unknown. Dredge hand, Dredge 6, 7, 8, and various.

John Tremiell. Original occupation unknown. Winchman, Dredge 8.

Bill Warren. Garbage collector. Bow oiler, Dredge 4.

Fifteen native ex-labourers joined the group, including Tom's mate Una Beel.

Were they the canaries in the coalmine, these trekkers from the gold dredges? Were the Japs waiting for them, ready to cut them down the way they had cut down the town? The company would surely not send out this leading bunch of evacuees if they were going to fail at the first stumble. It was talked about by the men up the Wau road, aloud, and they generally agreed that it would be a foolish decision. Also, Doctor Giblin was with them, and the good doctor was to be no canary, surely, so it was agreed that they were exemplars of this epic trip, not the sacrificial lambs sent to slaughter.

Wau and Bulolo lay on adjacent valley floors connected by the Bulolo River, which split several mountain ridges. Wau was 1247 feet higher up the range, so the river would always course towards the men in its north-northwest direction as they headed the opposite way. 'The bloody river can greet the Japs. We've got a plane to catch,' Lofty Burns would say.

But the elevation leading to each town and how hard the slog to Wau was going to be was the last thing on any mind. Mostly for sporting and social reasons, the nineteen miners in the party had all made the return trip at least once – but this was the first time it was a one-way ticket.

The native bois, one to every miner, whose villages lay on the ridges and in adjoining valleys and whose ancestors strode these trails for millennia, would have known every pebble on the pathway and had willingly volunteered to escort and carry the miners' gear before going back to traditional village life.

There was nothing else for them now. There would be no more waitman mining work. No more minimum pay day or free accommodation from BGD Co. The army only paid in rations, clothes and tobacco. Now there would only be waitman war work carrying gear and the injured and the dead.

There were only two ways to travel the Wau–Bulolo road: company truck or foot. All the men would have known that once you hiked out of Bulolo for a couple of miles the road made a three-way split. A track on each of the two ridges led up and along to villages atop both, while the other continued to hug the Bulolo River. It didn't take a committee to decide which road to take. The fastest way possible round the river road to hop on that plane and get out of there was the only route they wanted to take.

Both towns were mining settlements set up by two different goldmining companies; work in both towns was self-contained and therefore there was minimal business exchange between the settlements. The main reason for workers to travel from Wau to Bulolo and vice versa was for sport and recreation and social gatherings like the ever popular dances. The men would dance with other men's wives and with nurses. There would be a lot of doubling up and you would see your partner multiple times over an evening with the ratio of men to women leaning greatly towards the blokes. Tom had won ballroom-dancing trophies in Sydney and could cut a rug like no miner before him. He didn't play football, deciding he was a bit over the hill at forty-five to run around the park with the young fellas, so he enjoyed those dancing trips just as much as he enjoyed coaching the native bois' football team, becoming one of the pioneers of PNG Rugby League (which would become the religiously followed national sport in years to come).

Six months previously Tom, helped by half a dozen other miners, had trained up a team of native bois to play rugby league. It took some time to wean them off the *kikbol* they were playing, which was a bastardised native version of soccer with seemingly no rules, which the Dutch or German colonists had probably spread like a tropical bug. The Aussie boys wouldn't cop that. The place needed a real game. Not some European rubbish to corrupt the natives. In a short time rugby league was a success. The descendants of warriors who always thought of themselves as living links to this warriorhood since time began took on battles against other teams as if they were settling ancient family feuds. That was why Tom and his mates only held intratribal games. Initially they did organise matches between different groups but it wasn't long before bloody violence and outright warfare ensued on field and off, often with weapons, and the after-match grudges saw not just one revenge killing.

Tom would play touch football for and against other senior players and co-trained the non-native team that competed against three other towns – Salamaua, Lae and their destination, Wau. But that would be no more. With each step they took away from their town came the realisation that there would be no more rugby league or card games or billiards, or dances or socials. No more flicks or the magical working of wood in the workshop, no money flowing for the family. No Bulolo. No more.

From the moment the Japs knocked down their door, the unenlisted former miners who had to hightail it out of their town became the flotsam of war. After Japanese bombs and bullets wiped out all communications structures and wires, it was a level playing field as soldier and miner knew as much as each other: nothing. Fight and flight.

The NGVR boys the miners had lived among were pretty much all mates from the same adopted little hamlet. They ate and drank and played cards and billiards with and against each other. Miners and soldiers with no rank or hierarchy, except very loose nautical ones with the miners on the dredges. It was no surprise when the soon-to-be refugees were told in a casual town hall-like gathering that their town was to be annihilated. It would have been the community hall but for the Japs' extreme renovations.

Here they were in a ravine sandwiched by steep grass slopes, surrounded by the sound of whitewater rushing down. At a push the men could have made Wau in one trek, but the communal opinion was to take it a bit easy and do it in two bites. It was five hours since they set out from their town and it had been slow going even though they were walking on the open gravel road. Three or four of them had some sort of ailment that Tom wasn't sure of but they dictated the pace. With Wau possibly another ten hours trek away and having agreed to stick together to watch each other's back, they made where they were in the ravine the overnight camp.

They set up their overnight camp halfway up a ridge above the road and river still with Bulolo in sight, the airstrip forming a hallway carpet runner in a direct line between them, the town and the river. This did nothing to calm the nerves of the men, who were still rattled from the attacks and the prospect of facing who knows what up ahead. Opinion was that it might be a bit more mozzie and leech proof than camping next to the river, but Tom thought there was probably no such thing anywhere in New Guinea. They knew it was most likely the last time they would see Bulolo, because the next bend in the river that mirrored the road would render it out of sight. Soon, there would be no town left to see.

Smokes were rolled. Swags were too, laid on grass among the bushes surprisingly soft once the swag was squashed down with a miner's bum. The kunai grass was sharp enough to cut bare skin open but made for a good underlay. There were little clearings between the low bushes, which would provide minimal coverage for any red-spotted planes that may still be around. Roughly central to the swags, the fire would be sparked up.

Bill Warren, the garbo from Brisbane and Dredge 4 bow oiler, hung a blanket over a low-lying bush, his tent for the night. The truck driver Ollie Phelan peeled an orange and let rip a fart they would have heard back down in Bulolo. Will Marshall hacked the cough that hadn't had a break since they stepped out. Tom puffed on his durry and looked back at his town, thinking of the weekend footy match that would never be. The company, as usual, would have flown them up to Lae with the Wau lads for a four-way comp with Salamaua to kick off the season. That was the draw in place before the Jap visit. Giving those native bois the skills he grew up with and coaching them was what he was going to miss almost as much as his carpentry, he reckoned.

Looking back over Bulolo, the men could see smoke from multiple fires in rows, which had the men bouncing around the group as to whose house was going up. It was not celebrated when you won that guess. Then came the bets.

Jack Hill said, 'First one was Nev O'Neill's, right? Wife and two daughters all made it back safe, thank God. That one going up just now – see the first puffs – that yours, Lofty? Right near the machine shop?'

'Not ours, mate, we're up the rise a bit,' Tom said.

'Two fags says it's you blokes. Boney?'

'Not ours, mate,' David Bone replied.

'Show of hands. C'mon, Boney, Lofty, Phelpsy's, yeah?'

No show of hands.

'Shit.' Jack gave up.

Tom still couldn't think why he hadn't been permitted to stow the furniture he made with his own hands in the jungle somewhere. At least he had buried his tools and marked the places. They weren't going to steal his friggin' tools.

All the places they called home, some for months, some for years, would be ashes in hours. All bets were off.

A massive explosion that saw large pieces of material head skyward didn't need betting on: it was the power house. New billows of smoke from puffs to gushing black plumes had to be bigger than a house. When rounds of ammunition sounded up the valley like a major battle had just started they all knew it wasn't an enemy insurgence. It was the equipment stores with the discarded ammo being sacrificed. Fire flickered as house after house was taken by flame and smoke. The blokes down there knew what they were doing.

In very rapid succession, bouncing echoes of *boom-boom-boom-boom-boom-boom* tore up the airstrip. Smoking holes in a snaking line meant no Japanese troop carrier would make a safe landing in Bulolo anytime soon. Their town disappeared before their eyes. Tom figured by the time they reached the plane in Wau it would all be part of the earth again. He and the blokes would be the first point of contact with the world outside. The first to tell the story of Bulolo's destruction. But none of them knew what they were walking into.

CHAPTER 7

The Dark Cloud

PUNCHBOWL, 1942. It happened at every movie he and his mates went to. The inevitable and unmistakable trickle then clacking cascade of a lolly shell on timber floorboards. But only downstairs in the stalls at the Flea Pit Regent Cinema or the Astoria Picture Palace in Punchbowl. The upstairs dress circle had ratty carpet. And it never happened when the family all went to the big, grand Regent on George Street or the Hoyts in town, because they had posh carpet stairs all over, which was useless for Jaffa clacking. To compensate, the timber-floorboard-denied rollers would occasionally whack you in the back of the head with confectionery projectiles of all sorts. Jaffas were good because they were firm, but the rock-hard toffee sticks were the ammo of first choice, because they would hurt the most.

It was only ever Jaffas used at George's local cinemas. Probably because they were the only round, hard lolly made just right for this practice. And they were always launched at a heightened moment in the movie: just when the lips of a cowboy and a girl saved from the Indians were about to disgustingly come together in pubescent-tension-relieving comic timing. George, though, was finding the thought of smooching girls a lot less disgusting with each movie he saw.

Clatta-clack-clack-clatta-clack-clack-clatta-clack-clack right on the punchline in Abbott and Costello's *Buck Privates*, or a sight gag like them all falling out of the ship's closet in the Marx Brothers' *A Night at the Opera*, right on cue when Mo two-pronged Curly in the eyes or smacked him on the back of the head in every Three Stooges flick, his favourite …

'… why I oughta … I oughta …'

'You oughta what?'

'I oughta be more careful next time.'

Or any time in an *Our Gang* movie.

The Jaffa roller timed his roll perfectly, because it was maybe the fifth time he had seen the movie. *Clatta-clack-clack-clatta-clack*. No one heard any more words spoken on the screen for a bit – they were drowned out by the laughs and whistles and hoots. That's why no one ever rolled Jaffas during the pre-feature cartoons. Everyone needed to see and hear the cartoons. Mickey Mouse. Woody Woodpecker. Scrappy. Terrytoons. Merry Melodies. Popeye. Superman. Tom getting smashed by Jerry every time. The first appearance of Bugs Bunny playing Elmer Fudd like a fiddle. The other Looney Tuners Daffy and Porky and Inki and Sniffles.

The boys got a view of the world at war through the cinema cartoons. They had never heard of the word 'propaganda', but they sure knew who the good guys and the bad guys were in *The Ducktators*, and *Donald Gets Drafted*. *The Thrifty Pig* was the Three Little Pigs story with the Big Bad Wolf as a swastika-clad Nazi blowing down the pigs' houses while the bricks of the smartest pig were war bonds to keep your house safe from marauding Nazi wolves and handy to fend them off by throwing them like toffee sticks and sealing the bad guy's banishment. The good guys always won. They were always American ducks or pigs or rabbits or cats or mice or dogs or birds.

George and his best mates always claimed their seats near the front of the cinema to trap as many of the errant Jaffas as possible. They'd throw their jumpers or whatever they had with them in the path of the chocolate-centred red-outer-shelled balls, and share their capture evenly.

Every time it happened the boys laughed along with everyone, even though George often thought it was an expensive prank. Whichever kid was rolling them must have had a rich old man to be able to waste Jaffas like that, just for a laugh. But keep 'em comin'.

There wasn't a lot of work in Sydney, that was mainly why his dad was away so long in New Guinea and why there was enough money for the family to just get by. It was the reason his mum could always give him sixpence for a ticket to the flicks on a Saturday afternoon, and threepence for his favourite lollies, a caramel and chocolate Kurl or two and a peppermint and chocolate Bobbi. Or sometimes some Arrowroot biscuits and oranges grown in his back yard to share with Ron, Johnny and Keithy, even though the boys could still afford the lollies and drinks. They were tight mates. The Four Musketeers. Tight since kindy.

George's dad up in the New Guinea Highlands was getting a fair pay packet gold-dredging. He was sending most of it back home because he was getting free food and board up there. He only had to pay for beers and smokes. George suspected there were other reasons his dad was up there for so long. And maybe one bigger reason than the others. The girl. His mother didn't talk about that.

Some weeks his mum had a rare win on the gee-gees. There was an SP bookie who lived up the road. Most often on Saturdays, before the flicks in the arvo, George would take coins for his mum's bets to the bookie – usually no more than 5 shillings each Saturday in strategically placed bets over the day's races – and then return to collect any winnings and/or place the next bet. He was pretty sure this was doubly illegal, but he would do anything to make his mum happy. His dad used to handle these bets – always bets for his wife, Rose; Tom had never gambled in his life – from out of the public bar of the Punchbowl Hotel.

The thirteen-year-old man of the house would've got into all sorts of strife if he had followed in his dad's footsteps in the pub: boys and women weren't allowed in the public bar. And there would be no chance Rose Phelps would be seen knocking on another man's door, especially the door of a less-than-legal bookmaker. So, in Tom's absence, George had to do it.

Despite the money coming from the goldfields and any small wins on the horses, feeding and clothing and schooling four kids, with Mum in full-time domestic duties, still meant money was, as his dad would say, tight as a fish's bum. (Or when at the pub with his mates, a nun's fanny.) So, George couldn't believe that anyone would have enough cash to waste it on rolling Jaffas.

It couldn't have been one fella each time, it had to be multiple players, maybe even the odd girl. There were a few odd girls in and around Punchbowl. Some wild ones, but wildness didn't bother George. He liked at least three wild-ish girls in the district.

Anyway, you couldn't ever see who the culprit was because by the time you'd turned around to glimpse them in a moment when the movie was showing a daylight scene and sending a faint glow on the faces of the audience, the Jaffa prankster had blended back into the giggling mass.

Going to the flicks on Saturday after a footy game in the morning in winter was an all-afternoon affair. The cinema's cacophony became a mutual hush quite quickly whenever the pre-feature newsreel started up. Having been over two years at war way over there in Europe and the Middle East and other places George had trouble pronouncing that kept changing with just about every movie visit, now the stories about the war started to focus on Australia. A lot of people in the cinema knew someone, or were related to someone, over there fighting, so it was best to show respect and wait for the right time to muck up.

For some, this was the only chance they had to hear news of the war, and definitely the only opportunity to see pictures of conflict around the world. Big, stirring, patriotic orchestral introductions for the British and

American Movietone News, British Pathé or the Cinesound Review newsreel, 'The Voice of Australia', its kangaroo mascot momentarily enmeshed by the company's logo until it hopped off screen as if to join the audience and see how his fellow Aussies were faring in the deserts and jungles of far away and increasingly closer and closer lands. The voice that came from the screen was usually that of Australia's biggest radio star and therefore Australia's biggest celebrity of the day, Jack Davey, spoken in an urgent, nasal Aussie bleed to match the rapid editing of images to make the Japanese march towards Australia even more sudden and desperate to the viewer.

'With Japan's recently elected Prime Minister General Tojo whipping the mighty Nipponese war machine in a fanatical tempo the troops in Malaya including Australia's doomed 8th Division hopelessly outnumbered and outgunned have been pushed to the island of Singapore – there to surrender on the fifteenth of February with fifteen thousand Australian servicemen taken prisoner.'

They've got our soldiers, George thought as he watched the desperately cut images and listened to the sombre voiceover. None of this was going to be good for his dad. He stared at the screen. Bombs released from a plane's underbelly. Buildings on fire. Tanks burning. As George heard the words 'Australia Division—Malaya—Singapore doomed outgunned—hopelessly' he couldn't stop himself picturing his dad with his arms held above his head, his woodworking apron on and Japanese soldiers with bayonet-fronted rifles moving in on him.

His dad. The Japs had invaded up there where he was, and he wasn't even a soldier. They didn't give guns to carpenters – how was he going to beat back the Japs? It was true, then, what they were saying: the bastards were coming.

'The Philippines were in Japanese hands. Tojo was thrusting his trident further south, one prong aimed at Rabaul, the second at Timor, and the third at Balikpapan in oil-rich Dutch Borneo. And to complete the isolation of Java, the final objective on the eastern flank was the New Guinea mainland.

The dark cloud of Japanese aggression is spreading unchecked.'

The names of places he'd never heard before rolled around in his head; they were being invaded and wrecked. Australians were being killed and tortured, probably. Each time he saw a newsreel George would get a shudder waiting for Bulolo to be mentioned. Would he see his dad up on the screen? It wouldn't be a happy postcard picture of him.

The second newsreel had that Englishy, trying-to-hide-the-Australian-accent-but-not-really-succeeding narration – 'appairehntly' … 'fah fahters' … 'tairm and tairm again'. It would have been funny if he wasn't talking about the invasion of your country.

'Four days later came a blow which rocked our nation. The bombing of Darwin. The first attack on Australian soil …'

George watched as people ran along a pier and onto a road like frightened ants while bombs exploded in the water all around a ship that he thought looked like a prawn trawler. There were buildings on fire, billowing black smoke. It looked like the moving pictures he saw in every war movie. Were they actors? Was this real?

'The twenty-seven Japanese bombers which raided Darwin were escorted by fifteen fighters. They rained bombs on the north coast Australian town apparently annoyed at the failure of their attacks by sea. The battle of the Coral Sea badly upset their plans. Oil storage tanks ablaze presented a difficult task for the firefighters …'

A rough panning shot showed a sequence of bomb clouds billowing along a harbour sea wall. A massive black fireball beside a big tank: oil? George's body twitched at a trumpet riff he thought was just like Woody Woodpecker's machine-gun laugh.

'Every Australian is determined that this further violation of the soil of his homeland shall be repaid time

and time again until the Japs scream for mercy and then they'll get ... [long, dramatic pause then the next word with emphasis] ... *justice!'*

George knew that just across the Coral Sea was Port Moresby.

'Key base in New Guinea. Shiploads of war supplies are being unloaded in a hurry. For there is danger of jet bombers here too.'

He watched barrels coming off a ship and onto a wharf, but in what looked like normal speed and there seemed no danger on the faces of the wharfies standing round the cargo.

'The cargo is safely ashore when, duck for shelter! It's the alarm! A big enemy force appears overhead and comes into attack as the defending anti-aircraft guns go into action with all they've got.'

Now it looked real. Planes in geese formation. A soldier shooting an anti-aircraft gun in what looked like another part of the sky from where the planes were coming, the bombs peppering the water around the ship.

'The rain of bombs falls all round the unloaded ship but not a single hit! Through hell-like scenes such as this, supplies got through.'

The man's voice wasn't very convincing to George because it was sort of actory, but what he said made the boys look at each other and not worry about whispering. 'They're invading Australia.' 'They're here.' 'Told ya.' 'My dad was right.'

George and the boys didn't hear the plumby-voiced narrator say 243 lives were lost, 350 wounded, ten ships sunk and thirty aircraft destroyed. Nor did any person in Australia hear this. The government did not want to alarm its citizens.

George, Johnny, Keith and Ron came out of the cinema and headed out over Breust Place and onto the Punchbowl Road footpath four abreast. They were all off to George's place, eight minutes' walk away, for a late lunch/early slap-up dinner his mum was putting on. Three of them were still in their footy jumpers and shorts because they had a late-morning game and came straight from the oval to the cinema. Keith didn't play footy but he was a champion junior tennis player. George'd had the football from the game with him the whole time and now spun it upwards as they walked, then caught it and gave a quick pass to Johnny, who cut out Keith because he never wanted to pass and catch, and lobbed it to Ronnie on the end. If anyone was walking towards them up the footpath, whoever had the ball could treat the pedestrian as opposition and throw a dummy pass then make the real pass when the person went by.

'Your old man's right up in the mountains, inni?' Keith said to George as he threw the ball.

'Yeah. Right up the top, Bulolo. Goldmine town.'

'Japs won't go right up there, you reckon?' Ronnie said.

'Nah, I don't reckon. But they've got planes. With bombs, remember.'

'My ol' man was right, they gonna invade the whole Pacific, reckons we're doomed, reckons Australia—' Johnny was interrupted by Ronnie.

'Why would the Japs wanna bomb a goldmine for, anyway. Don't they just bomb ships and soldiers and stuff?'

'They bloody bomb everything, Japs. And chop your head off,' Keith said. 'And …'

'They've got soldiers where my dad is. Just a few, and they're part-timers. Volunteer Rifles, never seen combat. Said it in our code in his letters. You're not allowed to say anything about the soldiers or where you are, so we write like it's a footy game when he means something else. And he always says he's somewhere he isn't. He's nearly always in Port Moresby but he isn't.'

'Loose lips sink ships,' Johnny said sagely.

'And tell the Japs where my dad is,' said George.

They came off the footpath on the main boulevard and turned into the side street.

'Why no real soldiers there?' said Ronnie.

''Cause nearly all of them are fighting in Europe and they didn't know the Japs were gonna attack and invade so fast.'

'My dad reckons Australia is next, he does,' said Johnny. 'The yellow peril is coming for us. We're gonna end up Japanese, he reckons.'

'Should send up a crate of Georgie boy's old man's moonshine to chuck at the Japs like a Molotov cocktail,' Keith said.

'Shoulda never gone, my old man ...'

'Don't, mate. He's a good dad, your dad. Served already, mate.'

'Yeah, but goldmining. Jesus. Not away fighting. Never seen me play reps. Two years. Bloody two years,' George said.

Keith jogged a bit ahead and commentated like the league announcers on the radio. 'And the Berries are busting up the middle ... Burns passes to Porter as Kirkaldy chimes in with a cutout from Denton, no not Denton, he's fighting the Germs in Tobruk, on to Ron Knight ... spectacular! The Blue Bags've got no chance ...'

Ron yelled out, 'Car!'

'Oh no, just as he goes under the black dot ... in front of him, a bloody car, where'd he come from? ... oh, tragedy! Play resumes on the footpath, ladies and Germans.'

CHAPTER 8

On the Bulldog

It was like looking at a movie from behind the screen at the Regent.

It was the same number of planes doing the same bloody thing, five Zeros flying in the same formation, so they had to be the Zeros that had hit Bulolo. The bigger brother of Bulolo, the evacuees' destination, their point of safety, Wau, was swiftly dealt the same treatment.

Now, up there, the only way out was the only way that ever was once the last of the planes were destroyed: on foot.

Edie Creek lay in a non-volcanic crater. It had probably got minutely deeper over the past few years because the gold from there was dug from the ground and from the surrounding hills. As opposed to being gouged out of the river, which was the work of the Bulolo men. The five-mile climb from Wau up to their gathering had been more like fifteen for the Bulolo men once they had skirted in a haphazard semi-circle around the smoking mayhem of Wau and tried to duck for any tree cover from the mostly cleared ground.

When the last of the men had come up the path to the gathered group of miners and carriers, all they could see of Wau was the black smoke of the bomb fires sweeping up over the crater's ridge and wafting down the valley. They were just off one of the pathways leading into the tiny village, under some overhanging vegetation, so as to keep Japanese eyeballs in planes off them. This became an early adopted habit.

It was decision time. They were off script. Improvising. From here on in they were their own little scraggly army, though ill equipped even if they didn't face the enemy. The military decisions that had directed their moves since the first planes came would not come into play now. There was no one to tell them what to do, nor anyone who could get their story to the outside world. They were on their own. It was up here that it hit Tom hard. He wasn't going to tell anyone but he was bloody scared. He hadn't played serious football for fifteen years and wasn't a hiker or an athlete in any form anymore. Would he make this? He had recurring flashes of home. Of them without him. Doubts about the mysteries ahead.

* * *

The 230 miners had been formed into groups of fifteen to twenty and allocated their carriers back in Bulolo. They'd been briefed in a pre-hike assembly by the Commanding Officer, Bill Edwards. He told them all to pack lightly for the hike and the planned flyout of Wau to Port Moresby. They were advised to wear their mining attire – long sleeve shirts, long legged pants and boots and hats for protection against mosquitoes and sunburn. They were assured they would be provided with food or any medical treatment they needed when they reached Wau. How assured could they be, Tom had wondered, since there was no communication to or from anywhere in the world in their highland home. But he knew there was no option but to follow the directions of the military blokes who, once the Japs hit town, were calling the shots.

The BGD Co. had given the miners a cash stipend, to take with them, presumably to bridge the gap between their instant unemployment and wherever they might land. Tom and his mates weren't overly excited about the money as they had also been handed an 'I owe you' in the form of a contract, which meant they had to pay it all back eventually. Tom had acted as a witness on David Bone's contract as David had done for him. David said that at least the contract meant the company were confident of them making it past the marauding Japs and making it safely home to pay their debts.

Edwards told them that anything else they owned that was too large to carry on their person was to be left behind in the neat little timber cottages they called home. Tom already knew the plans to burn the town down so they all knew they'd never see their belongings again. Many would be carrying some gold on them. Tom wouldn't know who because no miner would tell another if he was carrying the precious cargo or not, nor how much in the form of gold dust or nuggets, usually in drawstring leather pouches. The miners had sometimes been given a small amount of gold by the company in lieu of a balance of their wage. There would be no way the gold would be left behind with other possessions.

* * *

As they had watched the destruction that burned below them – a carbon copy of their own town's raid – this small troop of bank tellers, carpenters, mechanics, farmers and men with no past agreed with a unanimous show of hands that the best next move was to follow the advice of the bois, and go where the natives told them to go – Edie Creek.

Even the miners knew that it was wrong to second-guess an enemy, especially the mysterious bloody yella fella, but Edie Creek was an abandoned mine from the gold-rush days, so knowing that the Japs had taken out the infrastructure and all air transport of active mining settlements – possibly as a supply station and barracks for a final invasion on their main target, Port Moresby – the men reasoned that surely the enemy wouldn't waste bombs and bullets on a place that had reverted to a traditional village, its spoils nothing more than pigs and vegetables. Surely the Japanese pre-raid reconnaissance had seen with the naked eye that the highland terrain was all sheer cliffs and razorback ridges devoid of roads and visible narrow foot tracks.

They had made it up to the village in the crater the long way. Rather than climb the steep, exposed mountainside facing Wau they had retraced their steps for a couple of miles back along the Bulolo River and then taken a path following an offshoot of the river and through a small gorge that looped around the mountain that Edie Creek lay upon. It offered less detection possibilities for planes that were still in the area and for those not having an easy time of it, a less arduous walk. Tom imagined what sort of shape they might have been in had they carried their own gear, let alone the axes and shovels and other heavier items some of the miners had included in their flyout kit. And how they would fare up mountains and across rivers in the ultra marathon ahead if this was the first couple of steps. But it was the native carriers, some of whom advised them to take the route they had taken, who lugged everything and would lug everything every step of the way.

Tom knew all the nineteen in his Wau flyout party, now the Wau evacuation party, to various degrees. Some really well, including David Bone, who as a fellow 'bachelor' (because family weren't with them) had shared a house and worked the same dredge with Lofty Burns, and with whom Tom had played bowls and billiards at the Sports Club. Alongside Boney were others who were close enough to know a few secrets about Tom, and about whom he knew similar, like Wally Head and Maxy Howard. Others were nodding acquaintances, billiard partners, dredge shift co-workers, and one or two he had never said boo to in Bulolo but since leaving their scorched and abandoned town had become unintentional brothers not so much in arms but blokes going up the same shit creek without a paddle.

* * *

Tom had bought his pith helmet from Reg Gillingsworth at the Company store. It was off-white, made with timber from the Indian sola tree and had eight canvas panels stretched and sewn over the frame. It had reminded Tom of those explorers of deepest darkest Africa, like Stanley and Livingstone, and as he was living in jungle territory, he'd thought, why not look the part. He never wore it mining. It was more for leisure wear, such as around the Sports Club pool and he matched it with his white safari suit when there were any outdoor soirées. Never for a moment did he imagine that he would embark on a journey that would rival that of Stanley setting out to rescue a 'lost' Dr Livingstone.

Tom's idea to start writing the diary notes on the helmet and a map on baking paper came to him soon after the men's communal decision to journey south down the native track. It would give him clarity and a sense of achievement to see each entry just as he had experienced it. Having blank space ahead of where he was going to write his brief descriptions and knowing he would need enough room for 'Arrived Home', instilled a small amount of purpose and hope.

The second entry Tom etched onto his pith helmet with his chippy's pencil was the names of the men in his party. Just the first letter of the first name, then the surname. Not the vocation back home or duties in Bulolo. He wrote steadily, in a line one after the other from the crown to the band. He knew he would have to write smaller and in very limited detail for all other entries because the walk across New Guinea and Papua was most definitely going to need space. Space to write whatever you called what he was writing on. Pith hat diary. Random helmet itinerary.

The first entry on his helmet diary, up the top on the right-hand side in capitals – 'WALK ACROSS NEW GUINEA & PAPUA' – took up almost two out of eight panels of the helmet. He knew as he wrote the names of the men down the helmet crown that the title might take up too much room, so his idea of creating a map with different materials that he could attach to the hat seemed not so silly after all. He had baking paper that had been used to wrap rice in. He had an ink pen. The ink-on-baking-paper map might also be a form of insurance: keep helmet and map separate at all times so if something untoward happened to one, the other would survive. Like the British Royal Family or US President and Vice President. Isn't that what they did? One could take over if the other was lost.

He would keep times and dates the same, but vary up the details a little. The wider, longer baking-paper map would allow for more detailed descriptions. It would be something to remind him of what they had done when they got home. He couldn't think about the alternative.

He was going to get home and shake his fist at the bloody Japs in doing so.

He and the others set foot on the track with fewer supplies and rations than the prospectors who had first come to this place. But the fact they'd made it showed Tom and his companions that it could be done. One foot in front of the other was the only way, all the way home.

CHAPTER 9

Kukukuku

It was simply a matter of history, topography, physics and tribal law that kept the people of New Guinea isolated from each other and why, because of separation, there were over 800 languages spoken on the second biggest island in the world next to Greenland.

Clans that traded with each other may have had an inkling of another's language through necessity, but the great majority of native people may not have known a word spoken by someone who lived even in a village in an adjacent valley. The impassable terrain mostly saw to that. Thousands of metres of vertical rises knotted with ancient vines intertwined with countless other species of plants no man could ever penetrate. For generations villagers would never venture outside their tribal boundaries. Everything they needed to survive and produce future generations was within the village.

Una Beel's Buang clan were from the north of the Bulolo River. The people of the Watut region were made up of a dozen sub-clans but mainly the Kaiwa and Biangai clans from the south. In between were the Hote, the Yamap and the Missim. Over the previous twenty years since the gold rush of the 1920s, up to 1500 men from all clans had laboured in and around the gold dredges in their river border between villages. The mining managers never put the men from different clans in the same working party; centuries-old warfare existed between the clans, and fight breakouts were unpredictable. The loyalties between the clans swayed over the centuries, so it was hard to know who hated whom at any one time. Best to be safe rather than sorry.

So it was before the *wokabaut* – the big trek – began. The Kanga Force officer in charge of putting the evacuation parties together had an interesting time matching the volunteer carriers from all the clans with the miners. And so, when the teams of miners and carriers set out, Buang only walked with Buang, Watut with Watut.

But by the end of the Bulldog Track every man would walk alongside the other.

* * *

The very start of the track from Wau through Edie Creek to where they set up their first camp was a common enough trek for Una Beel and his fellow villagers and Watuts who grew up in Bulolo and Bulwa and the Edie Creek surrounds. They traded with those from the village of Kudjeru somewhere in the valley below, past the rain and fog. This was, however, as far as the bois had ever ventured. In a few hours they would reach their camp in the village below, but after walking out of Kudjeru they would no longer know what lay ahead. Even though they were still doing the heavy lifting of food and supplies, they were out of familiar territory and could no longer guide the waitmen with any certainty.

While this new territory fell under Australian Territorial law, the carrier bois knew this was the land of the Kukukuku, the traditional enemies of Una Beel's people and of anyone who came into their world, including other Kukukuku in their own sub-clans. They were the most isolated of tribes, the last practising headhunting cannibals, and they would never recognise any law but their own insular war-based one. They did not discern between tribes, black or white, when it came to those encroaching on their turf.

Aussie and Kiwi miners pronounced it *Cookah-Cookah*, the American Dredgemasters *koookoookoookooo*, which made the local bois laugh uproariously every time the Seppos said it.

The Buang and Watut bois in Tom's group feared the Kukukuku, more so than each other; in particular they hoped to avoid the Kapau Kukukuku, the largest, most hostile and unpredictable of the headhunters. Sometimes referred to by Europeans as Pygmy warriors because they rarely grew over five feet tall, the Kapau Kukukuku made up for their shortness by their fierceness. They were semi-nomadic subsistence farmers and hunters who took on all comers, including other Kukukuku. They didn't trade food or goods; if stocks got low they would ambush and raid white and native camps, making off with anything they could get their hands on, their favourite target being all things shiny, sharp and metallic. Knives, tomahawks, cutlery. Raids would only be launched in the daytime, because evil spirits and ghosts of those they had slain were ever present at night.

The stories were legend. In the goldmines and the villages the myth around the Kukukuku built. Entering their territory made the bois on the move with the miners braver than brave in Tom's eyes. The fifteen carriers in their small group and those staggered across the track in similar arrays had voluntarily left family and villages; some, like their white co-trekkers, chose to evade one enemy to venture into another enemy's territory with the possibility of running into both and who knew what fate. All of them were on high alert as they marched on, one foot in front of the other and all eyes searching both sides of the track for any enemy ready to stop them from taking another step.

CHAPTER 10

Home

Every day she wore a cardigan Rose Phelps fastened six large nappy pins onto the left side of her chest. Some days she attached them to dresses or tops, but the cardigans always donned these outsized pins. Rose was five foot nothing and all bosom. From the top of her chest to the top of her thighs she was a continuous beautifully rounded shape, her upper body parts merging as one. The safety pins were always lined in a vertical row and had blue clips covering the heads, presumably to prevent them popping out of their anchor and therefore protecting baby's skin from being pricked when changing or when a baby rolled about.

The last nappy Rose changed was in 1941, for Ann. At the time, Tom had been goldmining in New Guinea for two years. Her son, George, was thirteen that year. But she wore her nappy pins on her chest for the next thirty-eight years, until the day she died in 1979.

They were the biggest, thickest safety pins George had ever seen, about the length of his hand, and he knew they would be the biggest he likely ever would see, because he once made it his mission with a couple of mates to go to every haberdashery and pharmacy and hardware shop in his world and he couldn't find any close to the size of his mum's pins. She must have had them specially made up at the Port Kembla steelworks, George thought. Or the Newcastle steelworks. They were about the same distance from Punchbowl south and north.

Rose wore those pins on the yellow floral cardigan she'd knitted herself as she sat in front of her Singer 101-4 sewing machine, transforming her eldest daughter's dress into a smaller version for Shirley. Tom had made just about every stick of furniture in the house, including the small table dedicated for sewing which could be attached and reattached to his dining table, upon which sat the sewing machine. The sewing machine could in turn be taken on and off the sewing table, which was always detached when the Phelps family shared meals. The Singer had been passed down from her mother in 1930 and was working a treat since Tom had refurbished the gear-driven potted motor before he went to New

Guinea. He had serviced all the appliances and motors in the house, shed and garage and had instructed George on how to fix everything as part of his 'man of the house' duties. George was glad he didn't have to touch the sewing machine and the other 'women's machines' inside the house – he only wanted to do the 'men's stuff' outside the house.

Rose had brought six children into the world. A son, Thomas jnr, had died three days after birth, and the firstborn daughter, Kathleen, died at sixteen months. A healthy baby was born in 1927 and shone love into the Phelps household. She was named to celebrate the way Rose and Tom felt when they looked into her eyes: Joy. Then followed George in 1928, Shirley in '31 then Ann in '39.

* * *

Six children. Six nappy pins. That's what thirteen-year-old George surmised, anyway. Always just there. On Mum. Badges of love she wore when she went out to the Club to play mahjong. Or shopping, or even staying at home for the day. Mum never gave a reason for the safety pins all in a row. George couldn't remember anyone outside the family asking about them either. But he reckoned that they were pinned where they were so that her babies – whom she loved living here on earth or in heaven – were close to her heart, always.

George had questions he couldn't answer and wouldn't dare ask. But he had evidence to support his recurring quandaries. The evidence lived under the same roof.

Ever since he learned about the birds-and-the-bees stuff from his mates in the Bankstown East school playground he'd had these niggling thoughts as to why he and his sisters all had different hair colour and degrees of straightness and curliness. Joy's hair was blonde and naturally fairly straight, made curly with Mum's rag ties; Shirley's was jet black and naturally curly; Ann's redhead curly. George was snowy blond, but was getting darker it seemed after every haircut his father used to give him and now his mum made valiant attempts to replicate. Barbers were just another luxury in this war.

Did he and his sisters all come from the same mum and dad? Tom often wondered if one or all of them were adopted. Maybe Shirley, because she was the only girl with olive skin and was the only one without freckles. Or Ann, because she was the only bluey, the only ginger nut. It never entered his thoughts that his mother and father could be united with anyone but each other to have babies. Just that there must be some other way to have babies and one day this big mystery of how he and his siblings looked nothing alike would be revealed.

Since he was nine George had seen in the flicks and heard in songs and radio plays, all this stuff about the heart connected to love and love hearts and people calling each other 'dear heart' or 'sweetheart'. Heartache and broken hearts when losing love, swollen hearts and beating hearts when finding love. When his dad said, 'Put your heart into it,' George knew this was a good thing with good returns. Make a real physical and mental effort when you take something on. Do whatever you do for the love of what you're doing otherwise there's no point doing it. There were other sayings he didn't understand, about 'wearing your heart on your sleeve' or 'pouring your heart out' or 'having your heart in your mouth'. That wouldn't be too bonzer, because you'd be dead. Your heart's got to stay fixed where it was when you were born.

Connecting what he felt to his heart was something George couldn't really work out. Pinpointing all this in just his heart didn't seem true. He felt a bunch of things all over, whether they were in muscles or organs or other bits, it didn't matter.

When he thought about his dad not being around he got a lot of mixed feelings, like when he lost something and then was angry because he couldn't have what he wanted and suddenly a wave of sadness mixed with terror mixed with confusion mixed with 'Why me?' would come over him. The latest newsreels at the flicks were giving him nightmares about his dad. And the fact that his dad wasn't there to see him run around a footy field was making him angry. Lost and alone, pissed off, wanting to smash any of the opposition coming at him for no real football reason even if they didn't have the ball.

The ache, whether it was in the heart or wherever, was real and it always happened when he was getting ready for a game of footy. And a lot of times even when he was on the oval during a game. If ever he scored a try, which was pretty rare being a forward, he longed to turn to the sideline and see his dad's upward stretched arms clapping and his smiling face in celebration of his son's triumph. But he wasn't bloody there. For a long time now. Too long.

CHAPTER 11

Topped Range: 7500 feet, 5.30pm

Tom Phelps and Lofty Burns had paired up from the start at Edie Creek and kept going like that all the way up the climb. One behind the other. Una Beel set a steady pace just in front. He wore Tom's pack on his back and had tied down a pot and a plate separately so as to not make any giveaway noise. He had fashioned a scabbard from kunai grass, which was tied to the bottom of the pack where his newly sharpened bamboo spear hung at an angle for easy withdrawal. Tom felt safe walking behind Una Beel.

They had topped the range, and it had pissed down from woe to go. At first glance through the mist Tom could see that eight or nine mining-town blokes and the same number of Indigenous carriers had reached the peak before them. It looked like Dave Bone had made it. Others too had partnered up and survived the hike to reach the summit above their first main camp in the village of Kudjera. Most were behind Tom and keeping the randomly segmented snake-like shape to their ramble. It was the only shape the men could form, because the native track – called Bulldog – was the width of just one man once they got out of the clearings and over the tailings of the old Edie Creek mine, making this particular jaunt quieter than most hikes Tom had been on. But then, those hikes had been for pleasure down the rivers and over the bridges near Bulolo. This was different. Occasionally he'd hear a word or two thrown over a shoulder to those behind, but mostly they all concentrated on watching where each foot went as they scanned the jungle on each side. No doubt, more to the fore of their thinking, to a man, was the dictum given to them in the pre-trek induction brief by the NGVR head honcho Bill Edwards: that only God knew where the little bastards were on this island, so leave any chat to a whisper and make it no further than a man away.

Even though Tom had never set foot on this particular track, he and his compatriots knew the nature of many other native tracks. Everywhere they walked, every bit of thick vegetation they brushed against, a Jap could be a foot away from them, an armed and trained samurai warrior who would run them through with his bayonet without hesitation. And here was Tom, a middle-aged goldminer with a gammy peg armed with no more than a knife he wasn't sure how to use even if he had the chance.

Even if the Japs were right up their bums with bayonets fixed and grenades at the ready, there was only each man's fitness and will that governed the speed in the one direction going up this, their first mountain. God knew how many more mountains they'd have to climb, Tom thought as he looked for the furthest mountain peaks against the almost-setting sun.

It was the longest, steepest hike Tom had ever undertaken. The highest he'd ever been. The haul had taken Tom and those with him about nine hours, all uphill from Edie Creek, with brief rest breaks in the villages of Kaisenak, Were Were and Winima, where they'd been greeted in a friendly manner at each stop. A good number of the bois were from these villages and it was understood the miners were running from a mutual enemy. Enough food and water was given to them to let them progress on to this point. And even through the rain, which had gone from the default downpour mode to sleet, he had never seen a view to match what lay before him in 360-degree glory. It was a day of many firsts for every man with him and behind him. He was level with the clouds that were clinging to some of the highest ranges. He looked east and saw cloud patches below their mountain. It was the coldest he'd ever felt in New Guinea, which made sense considering their altitude.

Parts of Sydney can be hilly but the only other mountains Tom had seen were the Blue Mountains west of Sydney. As far as he knew, it was still the place to go for honeymooners, young blokes in groups on long weekend buck's parties, or twenty-firsts, where more time was spent in the pub than on the hiking trails.

Tom's boyhood jaunts around the streets of Newtown, Erskineville, then later family life at Punchbowl, gave him knowledge of every hill and bump and small rise on his patch, but even on those he had to pedal hard on his pushbike going downhill to get any speed up. Nothing had prepared him for the Bulldog Track.

When he looked all round him at the encircling horizon, Tom would later think that they should rename those mountains back home the Blue Hills compared to the panorama before him.

Tom had never imagined seeing the world stretching on to nothing else for as far as his eyes could see but the countless saddles and valleys and folds of rolling emerald carpet meeting the sky, with no sign of human beings or any evidence of their ever being on Earth.

He felt like he had been separated from the rest of the world as he stood on top of the ridge. A feeling of isolation, an aloneness, even though miners and carriers were scattered around him and more were trickling into their rest stop. He was sure the others would be wondering, like him, what the state of play was with the Japs and the war that had put them on their path. He knew from talking with the NGVR boys back in Bulolo that if the Japs had made a major air, ground and sea attack with full troops on any European-built town in New Guinea they wouldn't stand a chance. Australia would not have enough troops to defend anywhere in the country, or in Australia for that matter. Churchill wanted all Australian military for Britain's use in Europe, just like he had sacrificed the Aussie boys in Gallipoli. Prime Minister Curtin insisted there was a war going on in certain southern parts of the Empire. Had they invaded New Guinea and were they already trekking on newly claimed Japanese soil? Were the Japs hoisting the Rising Sun on the Sydney Harbour Bridge at this moment? Broome? Townsville? Cairns? Or at their own, far distant destination of Port Moresby prior to a smashing of Sydney. The enemy could just as likely be coming the other way up the Bulldog Track. Right towards them.

They didn't say anything for a while, the two middle-aged miners atop the mount. Nor did the other evacuees and carriers sprawled, sitting, lying on their chunk of mountain. The vista and the communal relief of surviving their first mountain spoke volumes.

Lofty Burns had fixed the oil-skin tarpaulin between two boulders and made it semi-free of raindrops. He sat between the boulders with Tom and rolled up two Capstans. Without looking he revolved the tobacco over and over between his thumb and first two fingers on both hands simultaneously. Twin rolly papers stuck out from his third and little fingers. The only difference between the two hands and their artistry was that Lofty's right pinkie was only half there, the missing half probably still back on the farm on the fence where it was sliced off by wire that got him when he wasn't looking. He only looked at his work of art when it came to putting the leaf into their paper blankets, licked and stuck them as one and handed one to Tom, who held the durry up to eye level and shook his head in admiration at the symmetry of the cylinder.

'Swear you're a bloody magician, mate ...'

Lofty had heard it all before. 'If we were fightin' 'em off in Bulolo your old plates of meat wouldna taken the batterin' they just got Tommy, old son. No scrambling around like this caper. Just stand there and shoot the little bastards like rabbits.'

'I'm too old, too unfit to fight, remember.'

'Bloody 'ell. Mid forties, right?'

'Forty-five, just turned.'

'Half them bloody miners half our age that enlisted wouldna taken this palaver on.'

'That's the thing, Lofty. If I'm going to meet Saint Peter at the Pearlies, want it to be my way of going out. Not a bloody samurai sword knockin' my head off.'

'With ya there, mate. Christ almighty. Bloody knackered. That's one of how many bloody hills have we got?'

A pause as big as the next valley.

Lofty was looking in the same direction as Tom. 'Best sight's gonna be the mighty Pacific bloody Ocean.'

'A few rivers, then the Gulf of Papua's the first big water we'll hit, mate. Whole lotta hoofing it and who knows what bloody perils before that.'

Lofty dragged back nearly the last quarter of his ciggie. 'Just lost me love of a good view.'

'Looks like a lotta hard slog,' said Tom.

'Too right.' Lofty coughed and butted out his ciggie on the first of several leeches on his lower legs.

Silence settled back down on them all, as if the hive thought as one and refrained from using up much-needed energy by talking. The only sounds to be heard were the calls of what seemed like a few species of bird of paradise echoing below and the coughs and noises of exertion as others reached the clearing and set about laying swags on the ground.

They had agreed after an initial vote to make this stop on the peak for just an hour before tackling the descent to the village below and their first camp. A vote by show of hands was taken at the start of each leg, to verify the travel arrangements onward, and then a vote at the end of that leg. This was part of the ground rules the men needed. It gave them certainty and the sense of a goal aimed for and reached. The randomness of circumstances thus far and surely many more up ahead needed a democratic system. They weren't military, they were civilians and therefore there would be no orders from any one man. If time allowed, they would weigh up decisions together as a unit and give equal credence to anything any of the bois had to say. The system's main goal was a unified and unchaotic trip. Tom had doubts about that but said nothing.

It was only eighteen-and-a-half hours since they had taken their first steps of evacuation from Edie Creek, so Tom was surprised to see Will Marshall being carried by two bois who also had supply packs on their backs. Will was one of the last of the men up the mountain and was lying on a light-coloured canvas sheet stretched over two poles that lay on the shoulders of the bois, who walked with their arms straight down, even as they slowly lowered Will to the ground. He was coughing on a durry he held in his left fingers, and as soon as his body met the ground he leaned over one of the poles and vomited yellow. Tom noticed the circle of blood mixed with shit that had leaked through Will's trousers to the canvas as he rolled.

Will was clutching a small canvas bag in his right hand. Tom had noticed it at the start of the trip and thought his travel companion wouldn't have need for the contents for a while yet. All the miners had a bag such as this in various weights but all with the same contents: gold. Cached gold. At their trek induction speech they were advised by the BGD Co. boss to collect whatever gold they owned or were owed and take it on their journey. They were obviously not coming back to Bulolo, and it was policy to leave nothing to the Japanese menace. Especially older, sick men to torture and kill.

Will Marshall had the New Guinea trifecta, poor bugger: scrub typhus, malaria, dysentery. A shitful cocktail of some of the worst (and fatal) tropical diseases. His decline since they started out from Bulolo only days ago had been rapid. Tom had no bloody idea why Will was here and why the hell he hadn't been airlifted with the women and children and some of the very sick before the first of the Bulolo bombings. It was probably because he was hospitalised and couldn't fly when the decision was made to evacuate and, anyway, who knew the Japs were coming at all. Once the women and children were evacuated, they should have risked it, Tom thought. Will could have been on the next plane to Port Moresby and better hospital care with some of the other ailing townsfolk. Tom knew of at least three other patients from Bulolo hospital who were in groups on the evacuation walkout, with conditions unknown to him, and he hoped they weren't faring as poorly as Will.

Luckily the good Doctor Giblin, the first man in New Guinea to perform a donor-to-recipient blood transfusion using a bamboo tube as a conduit back in World War I, was on the hoof with the miners, and if anything happened that required medical intervention they couldn't have had a better man.

Blood transfusions or any other medical matters were something Tom and his miner mates left to the experts. There weren't any safety rules or officers at the mines; just the one-off rundown about being safe when they initially arrived to work, and then a bloke just had to be on the lookout. No loose clothing near machinery. If you did get into strife on the job, both the Bulolo hospital for whites and the native hospital were well equipped, and by Jesus if you could get the blood from one person and put it into someone else and fix them up, they were all blessed to have this doctor trekking the Bulldog with them.

Tom knew that Giblin was one of the best doctors you could hope for in a mining village, not only because he was also an expert in tropical diseases and conditions but he'd been living and working in New Guinea for over forty years. Indeed, Tom was amazed and full of admiration for the doctor being with them at all. He had to be at least in his late sixties, and like a few of the elderly miners he could have evacuated on the last plane out of Bulolo with the women and children before the destruction. But he chose to venture into the unknown with the men around him. A sacrifice that was never unappreciated by all the blokes.

Tom did have mixed feelings about the fact that it was Giblin who fated him this journey on the Bulldog Track. Like Lofty said, no amount of fighting in and around Bulolo would be as hard as the slog they had already done, and God knew what was still to come and for how long they'd have to march.

Will Marshall clutching his stash on the stretcher said to Tom that he was figuring out who in this black and white group of evacuees to trust to get the precious stuff to his family if he didn't make it home. Tom was dead-set certain it would be a white bloke because they were the only ones going – they hoped – back to Australia; and, well, you just wouldn't give it to one of the bois. They'd probably throw the useless stuff back in the river where it came from or cash it in some time in the future when the miners came back. And no miner arrived in New Guinea with any thoughts of giving up their gold for charity.

Giblin administered the most he could do for Will, giving him the tablets he'd no doubt been taking for months to no visible effect. He cleaned him up and scraped the chunks of vomit and shit and blood that the rain hadn't washed away from his clothes and hammock.

The carrier bois were already at the beginning of the downward trail when the men made motions to head off. Tom couldn't tell where any trail started or finished. To his eyes, there was no break in the mist-filled jungle growth. But the bois knew and wouldn't let them get lost.

At one point, when there was a show of hands, Tom saw there was a man missing. Leonard Schrater, a German who'd worked as a dredge hand, was nowhere to be seen. Tom thought back and realised he hadn't noticed him after they'd seen the destruction in Wau. He picked up his pith helmet and checked off the names. Scanning again he still saw no sign of the man. He hadn't known him but by now the faces of his brothers on the track were seared into his mind. He made a note next to his name: 'Disappeared on track, not seen after Wau raid'. He hoped he wouldn't have need to comment against other names, but looking at Will, Tom felt a cold chill. The track was no place for the weak, he already knew that.

Before starting the next climb Tom imagined the infinite view south for the last time, their destiny. He turned his head forty-five degrees to his right, knowing the sun was setting in the west. Wondering when he would see it again.

CHAPTER 12

The Girl

SYDNEY, 1939. Tom had bought his truck second-hand from a bloke who worked at McKenzie's timber yard. A 1934–35 Australian Chevrolet one-and-a-half tonner. Australian, because it had a body made by Holden at the General Motors–Holden plant at Woodville in South Australia. The engine and parts were first exported from the United States to Canada and then on to Australia because of the cheaper import duty when dealing with a fellow Commonwealth nation.

He thought it was funny that he was loading decking onto his truck to deliver to a builder he had previously unloaded timber for and from the same truck for his own carpentry projects. At the same timber yard. A kind of weird reversal of fortune. And funny too, that Fred the butcher was getting new decking on his house and he didn't seek

Tom's estimable carpentry skills. Maybe Fred thought that now Tom was driving a truck he wasn't doing any building or carpentry work. It wasn't true. Tom would much rather be donning his woodworking tools and knocking up a garden shed or a picket fence than driving all over Sydney delivering goods to jobs he could have been working on himself. It couldn't have been because of his craftsmanship. His work was good, he knew that and so did everyone who saw it. His bespoke furniture and cabinetry, the most intricate and finite of woodworking products, had added comfort and ease to dozens of Sydney homes.

There wasn't any head scratching as to why a lot of work had dried up: there was a war in Europe with its accompanying human hardships back home. Tom knew of his own family's boys who never returned from foreign fields. There weren't many Australian families unaffected by another war being fought under the British flag.

Bespoke furniture in wartime was a luxury, and Tom's lack of carpentry jobs meant his income had dwindled, and he had to do something to feed a wife and four kids. Even if truck driving was bringing in fewer shillings than a big building job, at least the kids never went to bed with an empty stomach.

George was helping his dad load the decking into the truck, which was a much simpler job now that Tom had customised the tray and the racks that held the timber, especially for the longer lengths of wood. The racks were fashioned along both sides and went from the front bumper bar to about three feet beyond the exhaust pipe and had six square open-ended units into which the wood could be slid; meaning it could be loaded and unloaded from either end without Tom having to back up the truck. The only impracticality was that he had to climb over the racks and timber to get into the cabin. Easy for George to clamber over and slip into the cabin. Not so easy for his dad. George was already an athletic, four foot ten, seven stone, almost ten-year-old rugby league utility player but Tom, at six foot and fourteen-and-a-half stone, found it a bit more of a challenge.

George put the last of the decking lengths into the racks and picked up his bike, which had been leaning against a stack of wooden crates near the entrance of the timber yard. No scrambling over racks and into the truck this time.

'Gotta get to footy training, Dad.'

'Goodo, son. Has he taken you outta the scrum yet?'

'Nah. Wanty's playing too good at five-eight.'

'Just show 'em all at game time you play a beaut five-eight. Or a nippy half-back like ya done before. At training too. Don't play like a piggy forward.'

'Yeah, but hooker's not too bad. Get to run a lot from dummy-half.'

'Well, you play where you're happy. And be safe on the road. Every driver's a ...'

'... blind bloody idiot,' they said together.

'Righto, I will, Dad,' he said as he slowly pedalled out of the yard and waved a goodbye without looking at his dad before making a right turn on the road towards Belmore Oval.

* * *

She balanced the cut flowers wrapped in butcher's paper, with books and vegetables placed in her bike's front basket that was hooked over the handle bars. A celery bunch sat on top of a copy of a book, *The Wonderful Wizard of Oz*, and a bunch of jonquils and daffodils were propped up in the corner on the left. She had put her nana's favourites, gardenias, on the right, alongside a bunch of white crocus held in place by a bag of large carrots and potatoes and second-hand copies of *Blinky Bill* and *Mary Poppins*. She read a book a week at least, often two, and if it was a quick-ish read like *Blinky Bill*, which took an afternoon, she would get through three or four.

There was no wind as she pedalled to her nana's house, cutting over the streets and alleyways and footpaths of this western suburb of Sydney. Still she asked Mrs Avalone at the fruit market to wrap the flowers higher than the petals to deflect the air flow created by bike and rider and protect her floral cargo.

As she looked down at her basket of goods she was taking to her nan's, she let out the first bits of 'Over the Rainbow', the Judy Garland song that was on everyone's lips and radios right now despite the fact the film had only just been released in the United States and had a year before its Australian release.

Somewhere …

It was the colours in her basket that had triggered her *Wizard of Oz* song moment. Even though no rainbow contains potato brown, celery green, carrot orange or white crocus or jonquil. Maybe daffodil yellow. No, it was the way the colours were in rough lines in her basket that made her think of a rainbow as she smiled and immediately launched into the song. And then she got stuck like she had for the past few days on the next bit. She knew the end couple of verses, the ones with the bluebirds, but this next run of lyrics kept stumping her.

… bluebirds …

'Oh, why can't I ever get that.'

She said this aloud as she hit a small pothole with both wheels, suddenly remembering she'd hit the same pothole on her last cycle to her nana's. Over the same driveway's gutter, *gadink-gadink* of the wheels and then –

… *dreams* …

'Yes, yes,' she said to the sky. Then the fast bit –

… *clouds* …

* * *

It was quite a feat to go through the truck's seven up and down gear changes and to push the clutch in a double-shuffle movement each time, but like anything Tom took on he was a quick learner. He faced any task or physical challenge as if he were competing against an invisible enemy. George had shaped up pretty much the same, especially on the sports field. Tom saw that every time he watched his son play footy or swim or do any of the numerous sports George took on with gusto. Tom never hid those moments of pride, occasionally shedding a little tear. He never shied away from those moments when discipline was needed, either. His boy was a good'n though. And he knew he'd got something right.

Tom cranked through the gears as he listened to his crackling transistor radio lying on the passenger seat.

'But to come back to the hush I said was hanging over Europe. What kind of hush is it? Alas! It is the hush of suspense, and in many lands it is the hush of fear. Listen! No, listen carefully; I think I hear something – yes, there it was quite clear. Don't you hear it? It is the tramp of armies crunching the gravel of the parade-grounds, splashing through rain-soaked fields, the tramp of two million German soldiers and more than a million Italians ...'

Tom looked upward. To himself he spoke over the radio. 'Bloody Churchill! It's on, isn't it? Ya gunna do it again, aren't ya, Winnie! Kick out Chamberlain, this time as the PM. Whack our good boys down the cannon barrels just like Gallipoli!'

'If Herr Hitler does not make war, there will be no war. No one else is going to make war. Britain and France are determined to shed no blood except in self-defence or in defence of their Allies. No one has ever dreamed of attacking Germany. If Germany desires to be reassured against attack by her neighbours, she has only to say the word and we will give her the fullest guarantees in

accordance with the principles of the Covenant of the League. We have said repeatedly we ask nothing for ourselves in the way of security that we are not willing freely to share with the German people ...'

The news was still on, the pre-war reporting and rhetoric growing increasingly strident. Tom was feeling less guilty these days about being just that bit too old to enlist. In his forties now, he was a Jack Lang Labor man; the older he was getting the more anti-Tory he became. We had to fight the enemy alongside our Commonwealth allies, that was a given, but Tom got riled when he thought that every decision made by Chamberlain was probably coming from Churchill, and Australian troops were always going to end up the cheap pawns placed in any theatre of war to make the Brits look good – or worse, sacrifice the Aussies to save the tommies.

The day was fairly hot, so Tom was pleased that the reconditioned radiator was keeping the temperature gauge smack in the middle of the oval glass dials on the dashboard. His apprenticeship and a few working years as a mechanic meant he could do his own repairs and get a little bit of cash-in-hand from mates and recommendations. Those had almost dried up too, though, from the very outset of the talk of war. He worried about that. About not being able to support his family.

* * *

She bumped up from the road to the footpath just a few minutes away from her nana's place.

... lemon drops ...

The footpath was newly cemented, she noticed, because it was shiny and clean and unlike the loose gravel footpaths on her family's street on the other side of the train tracks. Not even any dog poo on it yet.

Somewhere over the rainbow ...

* * *

Must've broken down, Tom thought as he approached a corner and noticed what appeared to be an empty bus except for the driver sitting in the driver's seat reading a paper atop the big steering wheel. Doesn't seem too worried, that bloke, thought Tom. Waiting for a mechanic from the bus depot, probably. Should pull in behind him and see if I can help him out. He let out a chuckle.

* * *

She had never noticed a bus stop where the bus was standing. There was a bus route down this street but she knew for sure that no one ever got on or got off where this bus was stationary a few car lengths from the corner. The corner she always pedalled across to get to the opposite corner, a block away from her nan's.

To get more traction on the driveway of loose stones she'd just hit, she pedalled faster and noticed that the bus wasn't blocking the driveway as she had first thought. *Gadink-gadink* over the driveway gutter and onto the sealed road passing the front of the bus. There was a man sitting in the bus …

… *fly* …

* * *

A flash of colour on the right and just below the cabin. Red hair, flowers. On a bike? On a dress?

Tom slammed them on but his brakes took a lot longer than the thirteen feet it needed to stop his truck. The truck didn't kill her. The timing was such that the right-hand-side load of timber careened from the top level of the rows of decking, and as the truck shuddered to its stop one hit her temple, her neck, her shoulders, her torso.

Flowers and vegetables flew into the intersection and formed a random off-colour rainbow on the black bitumen.

CHAPTER 13

Descent To Kudjeru: Camp No. 1

The emergency sidestep from Wau up to Edie Creek created by the Jap destructors was a common enough trail used by Europeans and natives since the gold-rush days when the Edie Creek gold discoveries were the first to kick off the rush in 1926. But the next stage was something else entirely. The newly planned route rose and wound up a mountain path, steep and overgrown in stretches, which made it good for a getaway in the daylight they were forced to evacuate in, lessening their chances of being spotted by the marauders. Alternative routes, such as up or downriver from Wau, offered no cover from enemy air attack.

Back when the men had reached the old Edie Creek mine, decisions were made and discussions had about their further advances. The decisions made were based on native knowledge and knowhow, but not solely. There were a couple of bushies who would prove to be handy in the extreme outdoors, like Wally Head, who would show he was just as good as any of the bois with a bow and arrow and getting food for his party. A good bush cook too. Tree kangaroo and possum were his specialties. Decisions on movement or anything else involving the group's actions were democratically handled wherever they arose along the track. No word of any plan initially came from any of the miners. From here on, the next steps were uncertain. The calls came from several bois who talked among themselves and translated to a few miners about a trade route deeper into the Highlands that they knew no white man had traversed. This was the real start to the Bulldog Track. Beyond the jungle tracks, cloudforests, and endless mountain ranges and rivers, they would make their first steps upon the alluvial plains and the coastal villages of the Gulf. All seemed agreeable that it would provide the best and least detectable path away from the Japs, even though no one assembled would know where or when the Japs might pop up. All the bois agreed the track would be *tumus hat wok for ol waitman* (too much hard work for the old white men), and that the threat of the Kukukuku was real, but he must decide. They would carry for the miners and guide them, and even though none of the bois had ever made the trip themselves they had nodded and collectively imparted to the miners it was *nambawan* – good. Good choice.

Mipela bai kirapim bilong mipela hat wokabaut.
We will start our hardest journey now.

* * *

It was an inauspicious crack at the next leg for Tom. The first waitman's steps on the Bulldog Track proper. With his shirt sleeves and trouser legs rolled up, it took just three steps into the descent of their first mountain for him to slip and fall sideways, sliding the full length on the wet moss of a fallen casuarina tree.

There was no bare timber or dangling vine on any living or dead flora where they traipsed. Even exposed rocks were moss- and lichen-covered, as if it were compulsory for every minute piece of earth surrounding them to be colonised, wet and slippery.

Of course Tom fell on the side of his tropical ulcers, and his shin and foot were already flowing red as he came to a stop in a thicket about ten feet down the log. Just like in footy when he got smashed in a tackle, he immediately gave the thumbs-up to the half-dozen men who looked down on him from up on the ridge to let them know all was well.

'It's roundabout here I'd a given up the goat, mate. How do they see a track in this mess?' Max called down.

'Stick close to your boy, Maxy,' Tom shouted back up the log. 'Here on in, they're gonna be our hope.'

'You or'right?' Lofty said and smiled as he crunched through the ferns next to the log.

'First white bloke to slippery slide down the Bulldog Track, mate. Congrats. You'll get a plaque.'

'Rather get a bandage. Una, mate, bandage. *Pasim*.'

Una Beel reappeared from his position a few yards ahead and stood next to Tom. He pulled the leather-bound roll of bandage and simple medical supplies out of the sack he carried and handed them to Tom, who started containing the blood flow and dabbing the sores with ointment before wrapping around the dry bandage. Doc Giblin was out of sight up on the ridge, yet to commence his own descent, but Tom knew the drill. If you can fix it yourself, don't bother the old fella.

Tom once explained to Una Beel that despite the frustration and fear that occasionally accompanied Una's attempts at some Western tasks – including using power tools or firing up the steam boilers on the dredges or even mastering English – if any waitman, like Tom himself, suddenly landed in Una's native world, the village of his birth, say, there would be no way he would cope. Surviving for even a short time without European comforts, along with the rawness of that environment, would render any whitefella a dribbling, messy failure and if the locals such as Una were not along for this particular little hike it would be doubtful if any waitman would make it out alive. The miners knew that. Apart from the staunchest of racists and the sometime abusers of the indentured native workers, of which there were more than a few, most white blokes up there knew that the inherent intelligence possessed by Una Beel's people would catch up with the experience and knowledge of miners like them, because they had seen it first hand. Learning curves from more than 45,000 years of subsistence farming to handling goldmining techniques were steep.

* * *

In the first few miles of the downward Bulldog, it was still light enough to see the abundance and diversity of life all around. Tom, his lower leg throbbing like never before, already felt as if either he had shrunk or every living thing surrounding him had got bigger. A green caterpillar hunched and stretched up a stem, so large Tom thought when it metamorphosed the butterfly would be the size of a small dog with wings. The palm frond it crawled up was relative in size to the dinosaurs that must have once brushed up against it.

The sounds without space. Closer and richer in the enclosed canopy. Multiple birds calling mates into the night's nest. He recognised the calls of two different kinds of bird of paradise. One of them sounded like a machine gun *tat-tat-tat-tat*, which got a couple of the fellas jumpy when they first heard it. Kel Austin ducked instinctively off the path under a fern. A couple turned to their bois, who would enjoy their reaction, holding out for a while before reassuring them with, '*Kumul, kumul*, bird' or '*Pisin! Pisin!*' – bird of paradise.

There was no pause in the orchestral clinking, clicking, beep-beeping beat of insects. Bass frog croaks trying to outdo all the other species. All this world under God's roof. At that moment, nothing seemed as dangerous here as stepping ever on.

They hadn't seen the sky and its navigable stars for some time, the slashes of light the moon gave them through the canopy enough for the leading carrier bois to guide them.

They emerged one by one from the thicket still in single file and out onto a slope covered with moonlit kunai grass down to a valley ring of open plain. Still the rain, but drizzle, so they could see a fair distance. He was about fifteen feet away and Tom couldn't make out who it was, but one of the bois called out, 'Kudjeru!' and pointed to the ground and then to a cleared path through the grass to what they could see in the middle of the open plain. '*Rot! Kudjeru! Rot wokabaut Kudjeru!*' The path to the village. They began their walk down. They used the fires of the village as a guide. They knew that this time the fires wouldn't be burning planes and houses.

CHAPTER 14

Arr: Kudjeru, 8.30pm

They grouped their meagre swags, passed to them by the carriers, in a reasonably wide part of the track that led into the village. Enough for them to rest their heads on their packs, to sit and lie with enough shelter on the vegetation fringes to not cop the full brunt of the incessant bloody deluge, under the biggest, broadest elephant-ear-shaped leafage. They remained just outside the village fringe in a show of respect.

A few of the carrier bois were underneath the stilted main hut in the village talking to elders, no doubt recounting the burning of the waitmen villages and all the friendly big birds killed by the invading big birds. The invaders coming to do nothing but evil, to kill and steal their homes. The passage forward for these men they carried for and their own safe journey back to their home villages depended on the response of the elders. That they would understand that these waitmen wanted to fight their mutual enemy but were not allowed to, just like the old men in the village knew when it was time for them to step down and the young warriors to step up and fight the battles. The time came for them to put down their weapons and be leaders. Relaying the information that this group were hopefully the first of many white elders to pass through their home while their younger warriors stayed behind to fight their invaders.

Tom and the others watched the children of the village, lit by moonlight and fires, run backwards and forwards to and from them, but far enough away to keep the laughter and smiles on their derring-do faces and avoid any danger from the ghost skins. A few women holding babies to their hips looked more like pre-teen girls. Tom could tell they sensed no danger as they giggled at the antics of their children. How strange it must be for them to see these white-skinned beings appear in their world, lying on the ground in various levels of exhaustion. Did they know they were actually men?

When the bois returned from the elders they were not alone. The headman was leading others from the village towards the miners. The wide, red toothy smile stained by betel cud and the hand gestures of the headman could only be interpreted as a welcoming party. There was a collective sigh of relief.

Tom only understood a smattering of the words spoken in a tongue that sounded to his ears like a mix of pidgin and another dialect and at a rate surely no man – even one who knew the languages – could follow. In Una Beel's obviously condensed translation of the headman's non-stop monologue they were told, first, that they were welcome to camp under the big house, *bikpela haus*, until they wanted to move on, and they could make small fires for warmth. They could eat with the villagers. The elders had seen the red spotted little silver birds and the big ones fly over them, towards where Tom and his fellow miners were headed. This was no comfort but the knowledge that they knew friend from foe was. Tom could only hope that the inhabitants of the villages that lay on their path ahead would be as friendly as these folk.

The big surprise from the chief was that food and a few extra supplies had been forwarded by carriers from Bulolo in the days leading up to their evacuation. Unknown to the miners, the Bulolo military were looking after the travellers. They had pre-arranged for food and supply parcels for the miners and carriers to be delivered along the track with each successive group, this being the first, and down as far as the old abandoned Bulldog mine where, if enough water was in it, the river became navigable to get to the Gulf and open water by whatever water craft was hopefully still at the site, watertight and available.

Here in Kudjeru, the first camp, no miner wanted to move another step. A few wouldn't be able to, yet. And some were in a bad way already. Will Marshall was still alive but he was breathing with a raspy rattle in his hammock, even when the angels laid him down with the men. It was decided the rest of the night and a large part of the next day would be for sleep and recuperation. Exhaustion stilled anxiety, and sleep came quickly and it was deep.

The general consensus was that if they made short, frequent stops they would only slow themselves down, and here they would have time to tend to wounds and dry their wet clothes by the fire that warmed them all night under the main hut.

At first light, Tom squatted over a dunny hole behind a tree near where he had slept under the *bikpela haus*. It was one of three latrine bogs they had dug just after arriving in the village. Furthest away from food and not too far into the open grassland. The men randomly volunteered to dig the holes. It was just whoever thought of it first. Often it was the bloke who needed to take a crap at the time, and who took the shovel and ducked behind a bush.

The Bulolo boys were never going to practise the open defecation that was the way of all the natives. Even the majority of labourers who had European toilets built into their comfortable company huts and had worked the goldfields for years shat anywhere in the open whenever they wanted to. Not right where everyone walked, but near enough. Tom would ask Una Beel why this was and would get: 'Where else to do this? We animals like *cuscus* like *walabi* like *muruk* – others that *pekpek*.' Others that shit. 'We *pekpek* too.' The bois were always barefoot, treading in their own and other species' faeces and walking around with the shit squelching in their toes; it was never deemed part of the deal to change it up for the waitman. The practice eased when the company began fining them out of their wages and rations if they were caught defecating anywhere in the township. Still, it was a hard one to police.

Tom wondered how long it was since a solid crap had passed his way, the friggin' malarial diarrhoea a reminder as he watched the magnificence of the sunrise up the mountain ridge. He squatted and streamed his squirts into the hole, a coughing fit playing in tandem and helping enforce each stream. As a way of distraction he focused his gaze through the sunlight beams clipping their way into golden strips of kunai grass beyond his toilet in the ground. The scene before him was beautiful. Bright green hills undulating towards their next mountain. Morning mist that looked more like ground-hugging cloud dotting pockets of land all over the valley. Stillness. He had always imagined native villages to be under some sort of rainforest canopy or encircled by a living natural force far bigger and more encompassing than a mere man's hut. There was always thick vegetation in his imagination, a boyhood stereotype of *ooga booga* savages in the deepest darkest.

Kudjeru lay in the middle of a valley. It was in open grassland. A stark contrast to a cold, dark, wet night before an ineffective fire, little sleep and coughing, moaning, snoring men.

Tom tried to keep his focus on the early light and faced away from the village and more into the tall grass and the green hills because it felt the safest. The humiliation of being pounced on and ripped apart by some beast from the jungle while squatting over a hole would not have been a good way to go. Tom couldn't think of which animal might actually attack him while he was taking a dump or what he would actually do to defend himself mid crap, but he thought it was a safer option facing the beast than it sneaking up from behind.

Just as he had finished his bush-lavatory business and wiped himself with torn strips of a *Sydney Morning Herald* that had been read before the war had turned them into refugees, a village man leading a pig with a vine leash around its neck gave what Tom took to be a good morning greeting and a gesture to follow him. He had appeared in the streams of sunlight from what looked to be a carefully tended food garden, and moved past as Tom adjusted his pants and belt. A younger man followed the pig. Tom fell into step behind the younger man and the pig towards his overnight camp. It looked like half the men had woken and were doing their first morning wanderings. All the carriers were up and about.

In a corner under a thick stilt of the main hut on a little grass strip, the young bloke at the pig's rear slowly took the pig's tail and wound the squiggly thing three times around his hand. The pig, not a big one in Tom's estimation by Australian standards, pedalled backwards and forwards in a semi-circle arc.

The Aussie miners who were awake and the few local bois who straggled from their woven grass homes gathered round the ritual. Most of the first group out of Bulolo were city blokes like Tom, but they didn't have to be farm boys to know they were about to see subsistence living close up.

Fifteen minutes out of Sydney in 1942 and you could hunt rabbits, foxes, goats and pigs, which would go a long way to supplement the family's war rations and put a meal on the table. As a teenager Tom had hunted with his cousin Harry and Uncle Roy and even dressed rabbit carcasses after shooting them. Rabbit meat was also sold in the streets of Sydney and announced to potential buyers: 'Rabbitoh! Rabbits for sale! Rabbitoh!'

In Tom's trekking party only Jim Hargreaves and Wally Head were not from the city. Wally was a grain farmer and any meat his family received came from the local butcher. Jim had grown up on a farm in the United States, he had witnessed where bacon came from. Ernie O'Hara was a butcher from Geelong, Victoria, but the abattoir took care of the gory, graphic butchering.

The man who led the pig had a cylindrical club; it was about the length and width of a man's forearm and was shaped like a wooden rolling pin. He motioned to the boy holding the tail to pull it toward him as he stalked the pig's forehead. Three oscillations, right, left, right, smashed the club on the bridge between the eyes. The boy with the tail laughed as the beast fell on its right flank not yet dead, convulsed with quivering limbs, blood pouring from its nostrils and mouth. Another two hard rapid smashes to the same area and the pig was motionless. In seconds the expert butcher whipped a knife out from his grass pouch and, starting from the base of the neck, slit a gaping cavity down to its backside. In a circular cut he detached the intestines and inserted his arms into the belly and removed the guts, holding them out proudly for the waitmen to take in, like a trophy he had won and they were a part of the sport. He lay the guts on the grass and turned the pig over and proceeded to slice one of a half-dozen deep cuts down the back from head to tail. The young boy had his knife and stabbed the full length of the blade into the neck, switched his grip and with jagged pulls on the handle, decapitated the beast in the same time it took to kill it.

Tom thought the slaughter of the pig, the cooking in the ground and the feast that followed might be some sort of welcoming ritual for the intrepid travellers. Una Beel would let Tom know before the end of the men-only sing-sing they were permitted to watch, that the feast and singing and dancing was part of a ceremony for a village boy in his initiation to become a man. This made Tom feel a little silly, but he was glad the first main camp had a friendly welcome, food and fire. He knew full well these luxuries and kindness were not guaranteed.

Tom could have easily stayed for many more days or weeks in Kudjeru, even waited out wherever the war was there. There was a feeling of safety in this remote village, however fleeting it might be. Everything they were doing was improvised. Everywhere they were going was a mystery. Running into the enemy or bad situations was probable more than possible, so thoughts of hunkering down for a good while seemed not far-fetched, but when the idea was raised, not by Tom, the majority of the group wanted to press on. The decision was made to spend the night in Kudjeru and hit the walking track with some fresh water and edibles, including some meaty pork bones, upon rising and then stick to the very loose plan of reaching the southern coast at least.

And so, before the sun even entered the village, the men got back on track.

* * *

The walking. Always bloody walking. And the toll was dragging them all down. Every muscle in Tom's body ached. But the aches were the least of his worries. The tropical ulcers had first appeared about six months after he arrived, but they'd never been as painful as when he finally got to sit on that first ridge they had topped. It was the first chance he'd had to take off his permanently wet boots and socks in the past week.

Seven days' worth of blood and pus and whatever other shit poured out of his boots onto the ground. It stank as if something had been long dead in his socks and had turned to a fluid state. How could so much liquid come from such a small area of wounds? Tom could only remember one gaping hole caused by the falling timber, but now he had four round, ugly, erupting volcanoes. It didn't look good and he had no idea what the days ahead would bring. All he could do was keep walking.

CHAPTER 15

Where Are You?

When it came to the newsreel stories about the war in New Guinea, the images on the picture-show screen only ever showed soldiers and their planes and trucks and weapons. On the march squelching through mud tracks. Letting off rounds of ammo into the jungle. Eating out of tin cans and smiling out of the screen like they were at Scout camp. Ships being sunk. Theirs and ours. Enemy planes in the sky. More soldiers with guns at the ready, trudging through the jungle paths. Sometimes George thought it was a really lucky coincidence for the man with the camera to get the pictures right when the action happened because the camera didn't move and the soldiers walked past the camera as if it wasn't there. Like in a war movie with the man's voice telling us the story.

The voiceover was plummy and Pommie, even though the bloke who owned the voice was probably Australian.

'The advance of Australian forces over ground just evacuated by the Japanese when Kokoda was recaptured and the enemy driven out. An observation post used by the tree-climbing Japs. Artillery brought up an inch at a time by muscle power through the jungle ravine known as the Gap. These guns were flown by fortresses from Australia to Port Moresby then in sections by smaller aircraft and finally hauled into battle through country such as you see here.'

Country his dad was hauling himself through? Country through which a man with a camera wasn't with him and God knows how many other miners. George was glad their fighting men were there and felt proud because the stories were always about Australia advancing and winning. He felt that without our troops there his dad would be dead for sure. He just wanted to see his dad's story up on the screen.

George never saw civilians surrounded by Japs, which there must have been. Just native carriers and stretcher bearers with the soldiers coming towards us next to a river. An Aussie soldier climbing around an observation post at an abandoned Jap camp.

No pictures of defenceless goldminers trying to stay alive as they were hunted like animals. No carpenters from Sydney shouting out to his son, telling him he's all right and he loves him.

Since the end of any news on his dad and the mystery of where the bloody hell he was, whether he was dead or alive, George was mad at whoever got the pictures onto his cinema's screen and a little bit jealous of the sons whose soldier fathers they knew would be safe because there they were with other fathers hauling the cannon up the muddy slope.

'Jap wounded left to die by their comrades are brought in by Australians out on patrol.'

It was the first time George had seen the enemy. The Jap. For three years he'd been watching plenty of Nazi Germans in the newsreels on the very same screen. The three Japs captured on film this day looked younger than him, he thought. One of them was sitting on the ground, uncontrollably shaking and blinking really fast. Boys with a stare into the camera that seared through George and made him instantly feel sorry for each of them. Shots of them drinking from a canteen with the help of one of ours, an Aussie patching up one of the boy's wounds and one feeding him his own food. Before that, George felt the whole of Japan was filled with the cartoon devils with the big buck-toothed grin, horns for ears and the writing that said they were taking over the world and wanted our women. The boys on the screen looked like they couldn't take a blanket over their body. Obviously they had been abandoned by their soldier brothers and officers, and that was another strange feeling for George. He kind of knew how they felt.

'*... Swamps, jungle fever, deadly insects and reptiles, tropical heat and meagre rations. These are some of the hardships which have to be surmounted while fighting. The daily dose of quinine comes by air. It's not asking anything out of the ordinary to extend to these magnificent Aussies our unstinted admiration. We welcome these pictures from New Guinea. They tell us things we should know as fully as we see how things are shaping in other parts of the world ...*'

If surmount meant overcome, then George could only think the hardships would be even more difficult to surmount if you were an almost-old man with other old men, bashing your way through the jungle without army guns or army food or medicine, without the help of what were now known to him through the newsreels as fuzzy-wuzzy angels. Maybe these angels were looking after his dad? Keeping him safe in their village, hidden from the Japs. That's if they were bush-bashing through the jungle at all. No one had told him where his magnificent Aussie was. Killed on the end of a Jap samurai sword. Had his head chopped off like some of the boys – the ones who weren't his mates – were saying.

These pictures from New Guinea weren't welcomed by George. They showed things he didn't want to see. Men going in to fight an enemy they couldn't see, with their army mates. Not running away or hiding. Not that he ever thought his dad was a coward; just that he probably wouldn't have had a choice. The pictures showed how things were in other parts of the world. Before his dad left for up there, his dad was his world. That world left him at Central Station in September 1939, and with no telegram, no contact, no nothing, George's sense of abandonment left the biggest, blackest hole in his stomach he had ever felt.

'... Take a look at the map in the region of Milne Bay. Ships of all shapes and sizes squeezing alongside the docks. With supplies which have to be sent into the interior the hard way. Patrols have to move cautiously because isolated parcels of Japanese are still resisting and have to be mopped up. Some of the hardest fighting was experienced here. It was a well organised attempt to take Port Moresby 200 miles away. All the paraphernalia of a force designed for rapid penetration. The late owner of the bicycle is now with his ancestors. The bayonet is more or less orthodox. But the bulletproof vest is a Tokyo novelty. The steel lining seems to be more for bullet deflection than

a direct hit from a 303. The respirator is just cheap and nasty. Two-toed rubber shoes are used by snipers for tree climbing. No praise is too high for the RAAF Kittyhawk fighter squadrons. Men back from Milne Bay say that the fighter pilots had it all over the Jap Zeros.

Now perhaps you'd like to meet some of the men who swept the opposition from the Milne Bay skies. Jap invasion barges now stranded on the shore with holes punched by cannon shells showing in their sides. To the Pacific the Japanese flag is as proud an emblem as the swastika is to Europe. We are not speaking astronomically when we say the Rising Sun has got to set!'

George only needed his imagination and the newsreels he watched to heighten his mixed emotions. At least the fear and the pining for his dad was heightened. Any hate he felt for him grew to become more hate for the whole bloody situation. There was hardly any anger left in him since the Japs entered the war via the silver screen. George could see a bigger picture.

Dad wasn't a soldier able to defend himself and his mates like a real soldier could. Despite the strange feeling of understanding he felt for the boy soldiers in the newsreel, George knew that the Japs were doing what a lot of people said they would do. They'd already bombed Darwin, which meant Dad was circled by the enemy, surrounded up where he was if not already taken prisoner, or worse. They had stepped foot on Australia. They had killed Australians. Dad wasn't with the people he loved. If the enemy came up Sydney Harbour or landed on Bondi Beach, which everyone said they would, Dad wouldn't be there to save his family. They were coming to get us, kill us, soldier and citizen. Didn't he know that? Wouldn't he come and get us?

The not knowing was the worst. Was his father still alive? Whenever the thought entered his head, an electric shock of fear and something almost like madness flitted into his thoughts. He shut it down quickly. But as time dragged on with no word, and the images at the flicks grew more real, the fear grew. Where are you, Dad?

CHAPTER 16

Camp 4: Will

4 Camp. 6hrs. ARR. 11.50 am

Abundant Fish. Olouri (Eloa River)

Entry in carpenter's pencil and ink on parchment map.

Our father,	*Yu stap long heven*
who art in heaven	*Nem bilong yu i mas i stap holi.*
Hallowed be thy name	*Papa bilong mipela*

It would be the first time Tom Phelps would recite the Lord's Prayer since he had renounced his Catholic faith.

He was an altar boy from ten to twelve, then at age twenty-four he made a decision that surprised his family no end, even though he had been educated at St Joseph's Catholic College and went to Mass every Sunday: unknown to all family members, Tom Phelps made the first steps towards becoming a priest. Out of the blue he casually told them he was entering the seminary. A carpenter becoming a priest. It had been done before. A bit more devout than they had ever imagined. More than most Catholic Sydney lads. More than his older sisters Margaret and Mary, who did not attend church, and his mother Margaret, who by this time was too ill. He would never know or care what his father Thomas thought about this or anything else. Thomas had deserted Tom's mum, Tom's world, Tom's family and was most likely getting closer to the heat of the hellfire Tom had wished upon him.

The Phelps girls got used to the idea of their Tom in priestly vestments and all the ceremonial delights they would witness. The thought of blessing a generation of western Sydneysiders grew on them. Little brother was going to be someone of influence.

Tom was on the verge of commencing training to become a priest when he met and fell in love with Rose Beatrice Challenor. Protestant.

No matter how deeply you fell for someone, you had better think through the decision to spend your life with a person of another denomination.

Divisions were deep. Protestant and Catholic. It was Us and Them. The Prods, the Proddy Dogs, the Happy

Clappers, the Bible Bashers. And then those Micks, the Bead Mumblers, the Papists. The Proddy Dog Liberals versus the Labor Micks. It was entrenched, discriminatory hatred. You would cross the street if you saw the other one coming the other way up the footpath, or cross over the same street to gang up and bash the bastards. To become romantically linked or even maintain a friendship with the Other was asking for a world of pain and hate from both sides.

To fool the Catholic Phelpses, every Sunday Rose would dress in her Church best and meet Tom and the Phelps girls at Tom's house and leave the Phelps's arm in arm with Tom to St Mary's Erskineville where only Tom would attend Mass. She would be a dead giveaway if she didn't go through the Church's many rites and ceremonies, and the Proddy Challenors would find out she had turned and there would be hell to pay on that side, so she would wait for Tom in the park opposite and read or knit and they would return home to Tom's as if they had worshipped together.

This worked for a couple of years for Tom and Rose, even up until they married in St Mary's Catholic Church in 1922, which was tolerant of mixed marriages for the time. Tom and Rose had two children who died in infancy. Then the Phelps clan found out about the Proddy Rose.

LEFT: At sixteen, my grandfather, Tom Phelps, enlisted to serve in World War I, but on the day he signed his forms, took his medical and was given an Australian Imperial Force service number his mother, Margaret, hauled him out of the recruiting office by the ear, scolding the recruiting officers for signing up underage lads. The Phelps women have never been backward in going forward.

MIDDLE: My dad, George, (*middle, top row*) in a school photo taken just before Tom left for New Guinea and asked his son to become the man of the house while he was away.

BELOW: My dad's identity card. These were issued to everyone during the war.

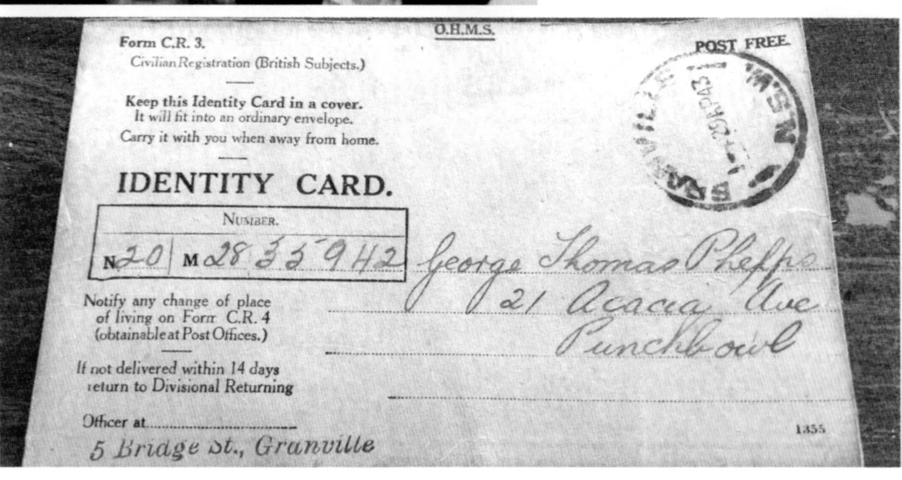

O.H.M.S.

Form C.R. 3.
Civilian Registration (British Subjects.)

POST FREE

Keep this Identity Card in a cover.
It will fit into an ordinary envelope.
Carry it with you when away from home.

IDENTITY CARD.

NUMBER.
N 20 | M 28 33 9 H 2

George Thomas Phelps
21 Acacia Ave
Punchbowl

Notify any change of place of living on Form C.R. 4 (obtainable at Post Offices.)

If not delivered within 14 days return to Divisional Returning Officer at
5 Bridge St., Granville

1355

TOP: In late September 1939, Tom travelled to the highlands of New Guinea, to the gold-mining township of Bulolo (*above*) for a three-year stint. The huts on the ridge were for the native labourers.

ABOVE: This is the house Tom shared with three other men. He had to stay in the bachelor digs because my grandmother had refused to go, choosing to stay in Punchbowl with my father and his three sisters.

TOP: The miners worked three eight-hour shifts to ensure the mine kept churning twenty-four hours a day, three hundred and sixty-three days a year. The only time the metal-on-metal pounding of the dredges stopped was on Christmas Day and Good Friday. Tom Phelps is second from the right, standing near the dredge. Una Beel is next to him on the left.

LEFT: The Junkers cargo planes, Guinea Airlines' pack elephants of the sky, revolutionised aviation and goldmining and made the remote goldmines the busiest and most productive airfields in the world. The planes were given the names Peter, Paul and Pat. Here is Tom with Paul.

TOP: Some of the men my grandfather travelled the Bulldog with. He is not in the photo, as I believe he was behind the camera.

ABOVE: The terrain my grandfather had to trek was almost too dense to traverse. The native bridges and native knowledge was surely the difference between survival and certain death. This is Tom on a bridge before the Japanese attack.

LEFT: Pop and his mate Una Beel. Una Beel told him they were walking an ancient trade route, a way the people of the coast, islands, floodplains and the highlands could come together. It was the only way out for the miners.

BELOW: This photo shows the men Tom travelled the river with, on their purpose-built raft. Again, he took the photo.

On the track it was the mud that slowed them down, and it was a huge relief when they reached the river and could walk no further. The prospect of crossing the river was less a challenge than another moment sinking down into the bloody mud. Or so they thought at first. In the top photo, you can see Tom with his pith helmet on. And that is him again on the beach walk, second from the right, once they hit the coast.

TOP: A vessel like the one that sailed Tom from the Mission to Port Moresby.

ABOVE: The ship that brought Tom from Port Moresby to Cairns, almost home. It was torpedoed by the Japanese a few months later.

I wrote this book to honour all those who trekked The Bulldog Track. But two men in particular – my Pop (pictured left, in his later years at home) and my dad, pictured below with me in the final year of his life. In telling their stories, I hope readers will know these two good men.

It was a perilous existence marrying out of your religious bubble. You didn't have to read the Bible or go to church to hate the other. It was your birthright. You would cop it for being born on the wrong side of Sacrosanct Street, they would cop it back. Tales of bigotry and discrimination lived on every street. A mixed marriage rendered families and friends torn apart forever. To survive as a mixed-marriage couple was a feat of courage.

Tom and Rose had been married for a year when Kathleen was born in 1923, Tom in 1925, both christened in St Felix de Valois Catholic Church, Bankstown. Tom jnr was christened by a priest in the hospital after his first day as he was not expected to live long. Kathleen died at sixteen months, Tom, three days, only months apart from each other and their grandmother, Tom's mother, who passed in 1924. Tom's sisters believed their niece, nephew and mother were all in a Catholic heaven and the loss of the tiny children so close to the loss of their mother was a tragedy beyond belief.

When Rose was exposed by the ever-vigilant religious police, the Phelps family swiftly put the children's deaths down as God's punishment for marrying outside the order. Masquerading as a Catholic needed God's retribution.

The fate of tiny Tom jnr's memorial was not known at the time, but for Tom's firstborn child's grave, its denouement was sealed.

The Necropolis Extension of Rookwood's Catholic Cemetery No. 2105 Section C, where Kathleen M Phelps was interred on 27 May 1924, lay next to the grave of her grandmother, and this would not be tolerated.

Tom discovered the desecration alone. The small headstone was upturned and an attempt to smash the stone had left marks of what looked like a hammer. The mound of soil was flattened to the ground and had been spread onto his mother's grave along with the still-fresh flowers. His anger was volcanic and he vowed over his mother's grave his immediate renunciation of the Catholic faith. His future children would be christened as Protestant.

* * *

Tom took on the reins of one-off padre in their little group not because he volunteered but because it was agreed by the show of hands around the fire of their last camp – and the slight urges of David Bone – that Tom was best suited. David became a mate of Tom's early on in the goldfields and knew that Tom had almost entered the seminary to train as a Catholic priest during the Great War. This, to David's mind, made Tom the best qualified to lead proceedings at the riverside burial of Will Marshall.

Doc Giblin withdrew as a suggested candidate, simply stating he wasn't Catholic and Will was. Tom had told no one he had renounced his faith some seventeen years before their camp vote. He didn't need to. He had looked at the face of a lifeless Will lit by the fire's glow and knew when the time came it would be a gesture Will would appreciate and it didn't have to connect to any of his faith's history. Even the Proddys said the Lord's Prayer. He made sure he showed no reluctance and had agreed with a simple nod to the raised hands around the fire.

It wasn't Tom's preferred outcome. How could it ever have been, a man without the vestiges or authority of the Church, his highest station in the Catholic Church only ever being that of altar boy. He was less qualified than Una Beel's mate Hawaina when it came to a religious rite of passage for Will. Hawaina who, with Gotokwa Benga, had carried Will Marshall in the hammock all the way to Will's terminus by the River Eloa. Truly angels. They were surely the best qualified to guide Will's passage to heaven. But the white man had to do white-men ceremonies. The bois knew that too.

Kingdom bilong yu
Thy Kingdom come,
i mas i kam
thy will be done
Strongim mipela long bihainim
laik bilong yu long graun
olsem ol i bihainim long heven
On earth as it is in Heaven.

Tom figured Will died about an hour before they reached the river camp, when Gotokwa had called out:

'*Yupela pren kus stap.*' Your friend has stopped coughing.

'*Wokabaut i go na stap.*' Stop moving. He stop sound.

It was then the track could not rightly be called a track.

It was miraculous how the bois kept him in his shitty pissy pus sling, especially down from the last bloody rise, their steepest yet. No one was sure if down was better than up. Vertical, always-wet slopes of fallen mossy branches that had the whitefellas slipping, sliding, tumbling like baby ducks following their mum on their first day of getting down and up a hill.

The incessant racking cough of either his typhus or malaria and the hellish groaning caused by the dysentery stomach cramps had Will constantly bending his knees up to his stomach in the hammock, making it even more nightmarish for Gotokwa and Hawaina to carry him. The hack. The fucking hack. The death-knell sounds were amplified in the echoes bouncing back from the opposing ridges. Hacks and moans that would have given any on-foot roaming Japs pinpoint accuracy as to their whereabouts. Everyone in the party hoped the Lord would show mercy. Sooner rather than later. If not for Will, then to save everyone else's arse.

In the last days of Will Marshall's life it was bloody awful to watch as all three of his ailments – dysentery, scrub fever and malaria – vied for their own crescendo. It didn't matter, but Tom wondered which horrible invader got him in the end. Probably a combination of all the bastard things he had and other things connected that he had no control over.

Malaria, which Tom had himself. The ache-inducing vomiting. Seizures. Nausea. Dysentery with the same violent vomiting and seizures and shakes. Scrub typhus with its added exhaustion, bleeding lesions and uncontrollable scratching that alone would drive any strong man insane. With the incessant coughing and vomiting and keeling over and scratching of purple welts, Will would have been praying not to wake up.

Tom knew that Will needed to be sent off in the right way. Peacefully and respectfully. This trip was always going to have its never-before-had-moments, its improvisations with every step they took. Tom knew that and led Will's farewell much as he remembered Father Joseph doing when he was altar boy at St Mary's.

Givim mipela kaikai inap long tude.
Give us this day our daily bread.
Pogivim rong bilong mipela,
And forgive us our trespasses,
olsem mipela i pogivim ol arapela.
As we forgive those
i mekim rong long mipela.
who trespass against us.

He was pulling it off but he felt a lot like how an actor must feel when spouting out lines. He may not have fully believed what he was saying, but he made it convincing enough for the others to go along with his performance. Being higher up on the riverbank's slope and looking down on the men added to the sense of ministerial authority and he felt it enhanced his performance.

Sambai long mipela
And lead us
long taim bilong traim
not into temptation
Na rausim olgeta samting
But deliver us
Nogut long mipela.
from evil.

Hawaina and Gotokwa Benga, who had carried Will to his last resting place, helped Lofty and Max Howard start to dig the grave, even though it would have been against their people's belief to carry out any ceremony with another tribe. This group of men were one tribe, at least for now. They chose a spot next to where they had come off the track, a place where the soil of the track's vegetation met the muddy, pebbly riverbank. Further enough away and a bit higher up from the river itself so as not to have Will float away from his final mooring at this or the next wet-season flood. The men took turns to dig into the silty mud and to slop it up on to the riverbank. A six foot by three foot grave was made. Every miner had a go at digging. It was just a random take over of the shovels from one man to the next. The wet earth making the load in the shovels gruelling and emotional for any man. Harder for men who had walked over mountains with a man they knew well and liked. When Lofty and Max carried Will and placed him where the river and the bank met the trees, each man threw shovelfuls of earth on and around their workmate and spoke a word or two in condolence, each shovel-load a blessing of earth and a wish for a soul rested. There was no chat. Tom couldn't swallow the lump out of his throat from the first line of the Lord's Prayer. Lofty had tears running down both cheeks and he didn't care if any of the fellas saw. They dug the grave between the big old roots of a Merbau tree like bookends for peace of mind. They inscribed his name with a hunting knife on the exposed roots.

The grave was simple, it had to be, they were moving on. It was deep enough for the limited amount of scavenging animals to not get to him and deep enough for him to became part of the tree's very self.

Kingdom na strong na glori,
For thine is the Kingdom,
em i bilong yu tasol
and the power, and the glory
oltaim oltaim.
for ever and ever.
Tru.
Amen.

CHAPTER 17

Bulldog

Tiveri. Bulldog. 8hrs (ARR 6:45 pm)

Time Spent Building Rafst [sic]

*Here & Dep on am 17/3/42**

Entry in carpenter's pencil on
Tom Phelps's pith helmet.

* *They had arrived at the abandoned goldmine Bulldog on the Tiveri River*

Rain would be inadequate to describe it. Rain falls; this stuff was shot by the wind almost horizontally and ripped into the men's faces like a thousand tiny arrows. Their eyes could only be squinted open for seconds before the arrows hit their eyeballs.

It was just enough to see the narrow and shallow streams that they had followed and crisscrossed in the high country, which had become a wider body of water when they hit the floodplain. It was still the Tiveri but it was here that it lived up to its name as a river.

They had stuck closer together since the rainstorm. It was sombre and quiet as far as human communication was concerned ever since Will's burial. The constant tap-tapping of rain on leaves and hats and earth overtaking any other sounds. Some blokes held on to their rucksacks on their carrier's backs as a guide. Some made sure they kept the clink-clinking of their billy cans tied to their carrier's sacks within earshot. Visibility was close to zero, and stepping off the path could be disaster.

The storm had got worse just about where the vegetation thinned out and the slope noticeably lessened, but still they had to shout anything that needed to be said for another to hear. So much for Major Edwards' advice in Bulolo about not letting the Japs hear you coming. Though they wouldn't have been able to see you to shoot you. Not even in the clearing the men had reached.

There was no rhyme or reason to ever call this torturous terrain a track or a trail. Tom could see no indicators to show that any human being had ever stepped foot anywhere he was now walking. Or any animal. Una Beel told him they were walking an ancient trade route, a way the people of the coast and islands and those of the floodplains and the highlands could come together.

He had also told him that inland groups only ever traded with their neighbours. And the Kukukuku did not trade at all; hunting, raiding, looting and pillaging had always been their specialties. Perhaps it was different in ancient times, or, as Tom thought, maybe this hell trip wasn't worth killing yourself for to barter over fish and coconuts.

The pace over the past hours across the floodplain leading into the clearing had slowed to a shuffle. The mud underfoot, sometimes under thigh, meant movement was glacial. There was higher ground and they looked constantly for any alternative path, but that would mean taking on an impenetrable, chaotic tangle of plants. The mud and the wind and the rain had meant the eight hours they had slogged from the last camp covered so little ground that John Lovett the boilermaker said, 'If and when you can see the bloody sky, more likely never here, you'd be able easily to see the last camp like it was at the other end of a bloody footy oval.'

It was the mud that slowed them down, and it was a huge relief when they reached the river and could walk no further. The prospect of crossing the river was less a challenge than another moment sinking down into the bloody mud.

Maybe because he was a recreational sailor from Balmoral in Sydney, Colin Phillips led the blokes to the lee side of the slope, where it was just a little less torrential and they could find partial shelter under some big, broad leaves. The leaves reminded Tom of the same plant he had seen back in Sydney as a kid. They all called it elephant ears. Col had been the fella who started up the sailing races on the dredge ponds using the simply ingenious boats, which were actually canoes with a mast, a boom with outrigger floats for stability and a jib and mainsail. They were sailed solo but could squeeze one other on as crew.

Anyone with sailing skills like Col or, even better, river-raft-building skills, would become leader of the pack at what would be Camp 5. The Bulldog Track had turned into a watery path, and since they hadn't seen any remnants of the old mine that had supposedly been abandoned twelve years before they walked to this spot, they didn't expect to find any vessels left behind by the pioneer miners. It was wishful thinking to even dream they'd stumble across a vessel once used to get down to the Gulf and meet up with the steamers that went from and to Port Moresby. Standing under the elephant ears they discussed how their next form of transport would have to be made by them, by hand.

From the outset, they had stressed the priorities on the trail, and what was necessary during a break. And rest and sleep, if possible in this cold, shitty weather, won the vote. They talked of collecting the materials from the bush around them and the building of rafts for their downriver voyage as the next priority. They would need energy that only rest would provide. Rudimentary boat-building would have to wait.

The wind had eased and the rain now fell straight down like it was supposed to. They attempted to start a fire knowing they wouldn't find one dry twig, and took turns scouring the old campsite. Later, settled as best they could, the men spoke of construction and decided they would need at least six rafts to take the seventeen men and fifteen carrier bois along with their kits and rations, and then of who would go with whom. There was never any doubt shown that this would happen.

It was in the first moments of rest, when the moving forward would stop, that the pain would really hit the hardest for Tom. When the focus wasn't on the moss blanketed rock slab he had to inch down or each step across that loose-gravelled ravine, an all over throb would hit him, followed by the knife stabbing in his leg ulcers and wondering if the next thing he ate or drank would stay down.

It was also the time he thought of home the most. Rose and the kids, tinkering in the shed, the pub and club and his mates, how his team the Berries had kicked off the season, or if they were playing at all with war closing in on Australia. But mostly he thought of Rose and the kids. Visualising them going about the house or grocery shopping, which he thought was strange because he rarely went shopping for groceries. That was Rose and the girls' thing. But plucking fresh fruit from the greengrocer's stand or buying a T-bone steak from the butcher shop on the Boulevarde and cooking it on the barbie in the backyard was one of the first things he wanted to do when he got back.

Tom did wonder if the family thought he was dead or possibly taken prisoner after having gotten news of the Bulolo attack. Even if they hadn't got news, either way they had no way of knowing where Tom was; no communication, a war on the soil they trod upon in a jungle and an invading Japanese army, Tom could only think that they would imagine the worst. And that George would hate him even more for never coming home and leaving his family forever.

It was about seven in the morning and rainless when they dragged themselves up and set about their allotted chores, like keeping the fire stoked or gathering wood or digging a dunny. It could have been seven in the night. And who cared what day? The men had needed to know the time when they worked the dredges because it was bundy on/bundy off in eight-hour shifts, but here, now, half the blokes couldn't tell what time of the day or night it was anymore.

Routine had blown up when the first bombs fell, and the men had been on native time since they took their first steps on the track. Essentially, time meant bugger all on this jaunt. Whenever Ernie Tomsett saw Tom look at his watch and make an entry on his helmet or on his hand-drawn map with the time and date of arrival or departure from a camp, he would mutter, 'Bloody pointless, mate,' or 'Where ya gunna use that, Tommy?'

Their journey was determined by the body's needs and what the elements dished out. Stop when you had to stop and couldn't go on any further; eat when you could with whatever you dug up or caught or were given in the villages; shit and piss when you could, or pray you never had to shit again in your whole life.

For the carriers, who were more in tune with their environment, even the extremes of the Bulldog trek were a part of their very being. The rain, the river, the tree, the bird, the man. To be as one with nature, Una Beel and the bois' families had 60,000 years of ancestry to innately turn to. For the miners, the Westerners, the waitmen, everything the elements dished out was alien. They were from a world that thought you could harness and control nature to suit your needs. All that was smashed, and they had learned quickly that where they were, Mother Nature was boss.

The natural forces would be crucial factors as they went forward, but so would the white men's survival skills. They couldn't rely entirely on the carriers' skills and bush knowledge. White man knowledge also had to come into play. To know they needed to start the night's trek when the sun went down and the moon rose, so that it wasn't quite bright enough for the Japs to spot them from the air but they could see the trail just enough to not fall down that ravine. To trek in small groups if they were in the open so they looked like natives hunting. Going native could save their lives just as much as the knowledge of what an enemy of the First World would do.

Una Beel was well rehearsed with the Western concept of time. Around the campfire two nights previously he had reminded Tom and told the men of a distant boyhood home and the ways some of his people told time, and how he still crossed over to that concept when he went back to them. With precise gestures to match, Una Beel had said: 'You put face uphill, yesterday behind you. You put face downhill, yesterday in front of you.' His gestures for tomorrow were the opposite pattern – the past is downhill and the future is uphill.

Considering their mountainous journey so far, this idea made more sense than checking time with a wristwatch. But they all knew their immediate past meant a great deal of uphill and downhill. Now, their immediate future would be downstream.

CHAPTER 18

The River

Gotokwa saw him first. He was standing next to Max Howard, whom he nudged as he pointed to a man standing alone holding a paddle in the centre of a small canoe on the opposite side of the river. Word spread quickly through whispered exclamations and nods of the head.

Behind the figure was a steep rise of thick jungle growth but even at a distance they could see he was wearing a kind of jacket with no front, more like a cape. His hair looked to be long as he had it up in a high bun, like a Western woman would wear.

'Kukukuku,' Hawaina said as the men gathered close. As they stood huddled together they saw others appear on what must have been a track through the undergrowth, and still more on the rocky outcrops above the man in the canoe. Tom started to count the figures he could see. Eight, nine, ten …

'They have hunting club, killing club,' Una Beel said to Tom and the others. It was then they realised the warrior in the canoe was not holding a paddle in his hand, but a weapon.

Tom felt his heart speed up as more and more warriors appeared. All of a sudden a forceful call came across the water from the man highest up and the last to appear. He was gesticulating wildly and seemed to be barking orders to those behind him. A couple of Kukukukus yelled something that the miners did not understand but did not seem like a welcoming cry. Their raised clubs underlined this.

The tension was palpable among the miners. Nervous suggestions of heading back up the track were quashed as Doc Giblin reminded them all they were in Kukukuku territory and Una Beel agreed it was best to stay put. They had to make peace with these hunters to have any chance of making it further along the track. There was no way they could outrun these warriors.

The canoe man started paddling towards them as the others watched, motionless. Tom felt like he was holding his breath and suddenly he saw two women, one holding a baby, the other with a child walking closely behind, step out of the bush and into view alongside the men.

Una Beel spoke loudly so all the men could hear. '*Meri. Pikinini.* Not hunt men. *Wimin with pikinini.* Kuku not hunt for men for kaikai.'

It took him a few goes and a bit of prompting from Doc Giblin, but Una Beel eventually communicated that it was not a hunting party because of the presence of the women and children. When hunting, the Kukukuku were known to kill and cannibalise, but this was men's work only. He also told them that headhunting was not as common as it was before the waitman made his country an Australian territory.

The tension may have dropped down a notch but they were all still nervous as the canoe man alighted onto the riverbank and walked towards the miners and carriers. His eyes were wide but he showed no fear as he got closer and closer. Una Beel told them all to stand still and show no fear or aggression and Doc Giblin said the same.

The warrior walked up and as he got closer they could see that the only other thing he was wearing, besides the cloak, was an arrangement of grass over his groin, held in place from around his waist with a band that looked like thin plaited vine. It was almost like a Scotsman's sporran. The warrior stood next to Lofty, reaching out to touch his white skin. Lofty jumped and the warrior's club rose slightly, but Una Beel started to speak. There was no real understanding between the two until Doc Giblin said to give him offerings, especially sharp, metal items, the most popular thing the Kukukuku were known to steal.

A knife and small axe were handed from Wally Head to Una Beel in a slow, unthreatening way. He kept them low and passed them slowly to the warrior. The Kukukuku warrior looked around at the group of men, then back to his tribe before gripping the offerings. Sounds were again exchanged and the warrior turned and walked back to his canoe and paddled down the river. Watching him, Tom looked around and the Kukukuku on the other side had disappeared, swallowed up again by the curtain of jungle.

'Don't know about you but I need a smoke,' Lofty said. 'Thought we were done for.'

There were nervous laughs and some bad jokes but gradually the tension evaporated and the miners and carriers started making plans, glad that they had survived their encounter with the Kukukuku. They hoped that would be the first and last time they'd see them. But the men didn't get much sleep on the riverbank that night, knowing they had given the Kukukuku sharp weapons.

* * *

The decision to travel the next stage by raft may have made perfect sense to the miners, any idea that took them away from that bloody mud was a good one as far as they were concerned, but the carrier bois made a different choice. They intended to keep walking the track until the river met the sea. This needed to be explained fully to the miners as it was already clear how reliant they were on the native men, to do this trek without them was a frightening prospect for Tom and his mates. Especially with the Kukukuku close by. And how they would find that meeting of the sea on craft that were yet to be built scared the bejesus out of even the hardest nut in the group – even more than the warriors had.

Since he had the best English of the bois and had done most of the translating on the trip, it fell to Una Beel to outline what should happen. He told the miners that the river would take them to the meeting place and that they were all going in the same direction. Even though he was a highlander, like his compatriots, Una Beel had grown up in a village on the river Bulolo and knew clearly from lore where all watercourses began and ended.

Una Beel explained how it would be best if he and his carrier team went by foot so they could front up to villages downriver and give them a heads up that a flood of waitmen were about to come through their village. Without a warning, the sight of a group of waitmen floating past might not make for friendly welcoming ceremonies and the men on the rafts could well be the easiest of targets for bows and arrows and spears, bunched together as they hoped to be on strange flat canoes. The Kukukuku weren't the only threat. The sudden sight of those men, whose skin colour they may have never seen before, could make the villagers question if they were human at all and give another reason to kill.

It wasn't just Tom who trusted Una Beel. He was universally liked by the miners and the other bois, even the ones from traditionally opposing tribes. He was listened to. Una Beel carefully explained the direction the miners should take and tried to highlight any areas of a river that could be a problem. And then it was time.

There was no ceremony, no goodbyes. It had all been said. The bois left the miners, walking in the direction they would eventually take the rafts, out of the camp and through the undergrowth, like a disappearing magic trick.

It was a brave choice from Una Beel and the bois to all venture ahead, Doc Giblin would later say around the fire that night. Doc Giblin reminded the men that their bois were foreigners, like them, from here on in. They would most likely not understand the tongue of the people of the floodplain and coast. They would be strangers travelling through unknown villages without womenfolk and therefore could appear, at first sight, to be a war party. Every one of them had some weaponry on their body for hunting purposes or potential conflict. Spears, bows and arrows, machetes, knives. It would take some diplomacy to deal with the people ahead. This group of armed men would be approaching homes and would not look like they were there for the hunting.

Left on their own, attention turned to building the vessels they needed to travel on. The jungle around them wasn't the high rainforest, canopy-covered jungle they had passed through multiple times before this point, jungle that was interspersed with open kunai grass fields and exposed razorback ridges. This jungle grew lower to the ground and seemed to have more varied species of plants than the Highlands, but it was just as thick and intertwined and grew right to the river's edge. Finding the timber they needed was going to be hard work.

Both Col Phillips and Bill Warren seemed to have the most nautical of bents among them and they assured the men in a circle-on-the-grass meeting in a clearing beside the river that the rafts could be made by each and every one of them. They talked through their ideas on construction. Logs should ideally be cut down with the three axes the bois had left for them and be two men head-to-toe in length and at least one man wide. They would need to cut and collect vines at least four-foot long, young, supple ones with small circumferences and flexible enough to be used to tie the logs together. The other main bit of the structure would be a long pole that would be attached to the stern as a tiller, for nominal steerage. They'd also need a few more long poles to lay loose on the decks, for digging into the riverbed as an aid for propulsion. There was much discussion and the numbers and dimensions were figured out on the basis that, now the carrier bois were hoofing it ahead of them, the seventeen men would need four rafts. They gave themselves three days to build them.

The Yank, Jim Hargreaves, piped up that the first item on the raft-building program should be finding dead trees. Preferably fallen ones, as they would have air pockets inside them, and thus would float better than live trees that would also cost them a lot of hours to fell by axe. Jim was a farm boy from Alabama with brothers. He let them know how any boy with access to a river or a dam or a lake in America wanted to be either Tom Sawyer or Huckleberry Finn so he knew what he was talking about.

'Typical bloody Yank, get one up on the Aussies,' Ernie O'Hara said out of the side of his mouth.

'Yeah, but bloody good plan if we're gonna stay afloat,' Kel Austen said back to him.

The first day was spent rounding up everything that was needed for raft construction. It was all hands on deck, collecting material for the rafts and bringing it all back to the clearing for construction. The sound of hard work, sawing, dragging, grunts and swearing filled that day but there were also shouts of joy. A recce for raft material had unearthed discoveries from the camp's past. Ollie Phelan had been hacking away chest high at a vine when he uncovered the V-shaped timber frame and horizontal top pole of a tent and, further on, on the ground, wooden slats the size and shape of a bed. This spurred on Len Cohen, working with him on the raft material hunt, to find more ready-made product.

Three more frames and poles and slats of tents that they guessed, by the growth all over them, were last slept in by pioneer miners ten years beforehand. It was a very rough guess because they knew how fast everything grew on this island. Ollie joked that it could have been last week 'the way things grow here'. These two blokes were very happy with their haul and even happier no axe work was required. It was like going to nature's hardware store.

Once they'd gathered everything together, the group started nutting out the rafts. They only needed to see a demonstration for a short time to get stuck into it. The industrious energy helped make the mood relaxing and jovial for the hours they spent working by the river's edge. They had a goal, they had purpose. More than striving to reach the next camp and making it through a freezing night, this was something they were creating with their own hands that could mean freedom and play a big part of their ticket home.

They found the triangular frames Ollie and Len had discovered handy when they constructed smaller tents on the finished rafts by attaching them to the decks and stringing a line between a pair of the frames before placing blankets as a canopy and putting their kits under them to keep them semi-dry from the rain. The bed base was used as a kind of raised bench, so very weary men could sit on deck. To have the chance to sit whilst travelling counteracted a fear of drowning or crocodile or native attack in more than one of them.

The way they chose who was to build and then be on board each raft wasn't like picking a touch football team, where the captain points to you or says your name and you join that team. In the clearing, the men just gravitated toward the nearest fellow or the bloke he knew he'd get along with.

It turned out that Tom would be on a six-man raft with Max Howard, David Bone, Jim Hargreaves, Jack Hill and

Doc Giblin. The other three rafts would have five and four and two men per raft, the four- and two-man vessels also transporting all the food supply and a majority of the swags, blankets, pots, plates and billy tins.

Tom's group was the first to launch from the rotting remnants of the original miners' jetty, which was now basically just four poles poking out of the water at various angles next to the bank. From here, four newly minted rafts, that would definitely not win any nautical beauty contests, were tied up with vine. Everything was tied up with vine. Tom and his crew on raft number one were bon voyaged, with a smashing of a billy tin filled with river water substituting for champagne, and a hail of salutations – 'See you at the sea!' 'Bon voyage!' 'God bless all who sail on her!' 'Fair wind and good fortune!'

The more over the top the better the laugh. It was all seen as especially humorous because it was slow floating to begin with, as Dave and Tom were both on the port side using poles to push them along close to shore. They'd only reached mid-stream some half an hour after launch, still listening to intermittent encouragement shouted from the others on shore preparing for their own launch.

* * *

Five hours later, the crew of the *Bulolo Babe*, as they had called their ugly duckling, were getting accustomed to the movement atop the surface of the flowing river. They'd launched on the Tiveri River at Bulldog and the water course had now become the Lakekamu. It was much wider and deeper, with bend after bend after bend, an endless snake. In pairs, they took turns standing on either side of the raft, paddling in unison with the handcrafted poles. The only crew member not on paddling shift was Doc Giblin. He was an elderly man who had done enough for the health and wellbeing of the men to be afforded a rest up.

The raft was faring well, the water was at a good level, forming a semi-circle across the top of the logs, which Big Jim the Yankee raft expert said was a good sign of flotation. The vine bindings only required tightening here and there if they were seen to be trailing in the water. They had a feed of the rations at random intervals, the tobacco and matches were still dry and the chat was leisurely, mostly about life before mining. Tom found out more about all of his raft mates in the first half-day float than he had in three years of working alongside them. If it was like this to the coast, it would be just fine by all on board.

As the river narrowed after another hour Jack Hill, who was on the tiller, spotted something ahead, which was moving towards them at ten o'clock.

'That log, mate. It's got eyes.'

'I thought it was floating the wrong way upriver,' Tom said.

'Get into the centre, fellas. Two of us grab a pole and get on either end. Poke the bastard in the eye if he has a leap,' was Max Howard's solution.

'Ya kiddin' right. That'll just piss him off more,' said Dave Bone.

'Has a leap! Do they leap? Jesus H Christ!' Big Jim the Yank hadn't experienced this as Huck Finn. Huck only had to deal with alligators.

'Johnny Lovett's got the only rifle. How far back would he be?' queried Jack. No one answered because it wouldn't have made any bloody difference. They couldn't go back with no motor, and the others couldn't go any faster forward.

Doc Giblin was the voice of reason. 'A crocodile wouldn't have seen such a thing as this before. Hopefully he's just curious. Being in the middle of our ship would seem a good idea, yes. No dangling legs, gents. I don't have that kind of medical aid I'm afraid.'

The six men steadied themselves and stared at the log with eyes, that frozenly stared back, the tail visible and s-bending closer. Max had the pole raised, aimed ready to strike. Within ten feet the croc stopped his swim and floated sideways at the speed of the raft for ten minutes or so. Slowly he submerged until his eyes and nostrils were replaced by bubbles. All, except Jack on the tiller playing skipper, kept looking behind their craft at where they had seen the croc last. They were still looking backwards and forwards, scanning the surface ready for a leap, when Jack noticed the craft had picked up speed quickly.

'Hold onto the decks, lads,' the skipper of the hour said, trying not to raise panic levels. Within a couple of minutes they were up and down small rises and dips and the water was turning white. Jack had virtually zero control of the tiller so he couldn't steer around the first rock that appeared jutting out of the water. The raft's bow looked to be headed square into the centre of it when a dip down the small swell just before certain collision skew-whiffed the raft and sent it sideways, punting it broadside against the boulder, smashing one of the tent frames of the makeshift shelter and sending it into the water. They all held onto the centre logs, Tom with one arm around the back of the doctor. The raft was holding in place against the rock, just, waves slapping rhythmically over the side drenching all of them ... And where was that damn croc!

* * *

There was no sign of the croc but their luck had run out after dodging overhanging tree branches and vine snags along the banks and from logs and rocks underwater. The combination of collisions and scrapes into protruding rocks, sand bars and a couple of jagged rock outcrops had rendered them to a standstill, shipwrecked in the middle of the river.

The six were still together, sitting or standing on the raft near the end of the rapids. A log ahead of them in the white water had speared lengthwise into a small rocky outcrop, one of the dozens they had got around by fending off or steering with their poles. Another log had struck the one in the outcrop of rocks and formed an inverted 'T' and created a perfect crashing point. The raft hit the logs and jackknifed the stern into the air. The first things to fly off the raft were the canvas bags of food and flasks of water, rations which would have sustained them for a few more days, fish caught at the raft-building camp, rice, sugar cane stalks and balls of sago. As soon as the rations slid into the water they sank beneath the whitewater, out of reach. The next object propelled off the raft was Jack Hill, who had gotten back onto the pole tiller as the steerer. He was catapulted sideways on impact with the logs and rocks. Then it was Jim Hargreaves who shot into the water a few seconds after Jack. Jim managed to go with the flow of the rapids and was the first to reach the deeper, slower moving part of the river and the first to make it onto a little island of soon-to-be castaways by swimming breaststroke, signalling for others a passage of relative safety. He must've played Huck Finn a fair bit, Tom would say to Jim later on the island beach. Tom assumed his role of protector of Doc Giblin, as he managed to hold onto the bindings of two of the logs that remained beneath him to pull the Doc belly down and perpendicular to the logs. It was getting closer to slower, deeper water and Dave Bone and Max Howard had a log each, riding the end of the logs by hugging their ends and trailing their feet in the water, doing the right thing by not fighting against the rushing river and moving forward. Jack Hill would thank his lucky stars as well as his fifteen years rescuing people in a surf belt as a lifesaver at Maroubra when he body surfed the whitewater and dodged obstacles using the head-out-of-water freestyle approach you needed to master in a surf race. Once he exited the rapids he swam to Max, who was still embracing a log. His instincts drew him to Max as being the one in most need of help, just like he would spot a swimmer in trouble in a rip. Max was joined by Jack, getting a hold on the log and being assured he was okay with a thumbs up and a 'this wasn't in the briefing old son'. Dave was now lying belly down on his log and Tom and Doc Giblin were a couple of log lengths away, all of them in the middle of the stream and floating towards the sand island that Jim was willing them to reach. Except perhaps for Jack, who was still reasonably surf fit, the men were in no state to battle the current and had to let the river take them where it wished.

* * *

They spent two days on the sandy river island. Two days without food. None of the six men were willing to risk the swim to the bank on either side. Even Jack the lifesaver knew they were all too sick or exhausted to swim to the riverbank or stay afloat and paddle on the logs over the deep, wide water. If by chance one did make it, what would he do once he made it to shore? He would need watercraft and help to rescue his fellow castaways. No, they would keep their pact of never going solo. Best to wait for the other miners heading downriver and hitch a ride to the river mouth when they arrived, if they arrived. But it was three days since they had seen anyone from their trekking group. No miners on rafts were seen coming around that last bend in the river towards them, or any carrier bois on foot, walking down the river's bushside tracks and beaches. They concocted theories on why it was taking the other miners so long to get there as they lazed on the little island, weighing up options. Lazed because they could do little else in a space the size of two rooms of a house. And the truth was, they were too stuffed to do anything requiring physical activity.

They had no idea where the other groups were. Had they decided to delay their trips? Waited for the dozens reaching the latest stage of their journey to come en masse? Crazy move, someone said. They would be sitting ducks on an open river. Wasn't that the reason they had split into groups in the first place. Perhaps they'd decided to walk to the ocean like the carriers? Had they met with a roaming Kukukuku clan and thus been attacked? They would have heard, surely, the angry bee buzzing of the Jap Zeros coming in for other attacks. But where were the rest of them? All they could do was wait. Though they weren't sure for what.

* * *

'Is that a friggin' plane?' Max said with alarm, responding to the distant pulsing *putta-putta-putta* that could have easily been the buzz of a Zero's approach. All the sounds they heard on this caper were foreign and often distorted in their ears by forest canopy and echoey mountain ranges and rivers. *Putta-putta-putta*.

'Sounds too slow', David said, as they each turned their heads back and forth, attempting to match the buzz with the visual.

Jim the Yank put in his two bob's worth. 'Don't reckon that's in the sky,' he said.

'We're fucked sitting on this bullseye of an island if it is,' said Jack.

If anyone was coming their way they thought it would surely come from upriver, where they had streamed down from.

'It's a boat motor,' Tom said, the first to stand up from their beach and turn to the south.

'Think you're right,' said Jack. 'Coming upriver.'

A motor boat wasn't what they saw coming round the bend, though. The needle-shaped tip of a canoe and first one, then two paddlers, native fellows, one on the bow and one on the stern, another canoe on the first one's tail, nudging around the river bend. And then the source of the engine noise, accompanied by two more long canoes paddling at the same speed, a half-cabin motor boat delivering the diesel *putta-putta-putta* of the launch. A launch being piloted by a white man standing at the wheel in a long black coat. Tom knew straight away it was a priest.

For a few seconds Tom thought what was gliding towards him on the river and the other blokes must be a mirage, a Catholic-themed hallucination brought on by the hunger pains all of them were going through or something he'd seen once in a jungle movie.

'We get you home, bos!' Una Beel shouted out to him. This was no mirage. There he was in the front of the canoe travelling alongside the launch, waving a paddle. 'We get all home!'

The four canoes and the motor boat reached them fairly quickly considering they were going against the flow of the river.

The five vessels slid smoothly onto the sand, taking up the length of the tiny island's beach. Gotokwa and Hawaina, the carriers who'd stretchered Will Marshall all those miles over the track, were in the rescue party and joined the men on the beach with the priest who, after greetings were made in very broken English, opened out a sack on the sand which had chunks of bread, cans of fruit and containers of water. This priest was definitely answering the prayers of the stranded six.

CHAPTER 19

Punchbowl Telegram

Her eldest girl, Joy, sat opposite Rose, hand stitching two lengths of red rags she'd found in Tom's shed. As her mother sewed, three-year-old Anne was under the table chasing a ball of wool she had thrown, competing with the cat in a game she could never win because the cat was too fast and was playing another game. Pounce and trap. Not throw, chase and retrieve.

Rose's middle girl, Shirley, was standing at the side of the bay window looking out at the boys on the street. Joy held up the faded red 'V' to her mother that she had fashioned with a needle and thread. Just as she did, she saw beyond the 'V' through the window to her brother George and his friends.

Out on the street Ron Jorgenson had the cricket bat and was showing off again, still trying to hook a six into the window Shirley was looking out. Johnny Want and Keith Jones were throwing balls at Ron, French-cricket style, even though Ron's stance was the conventional cricket pose. You couldn't hit it as far as the windows of the houses if you did the straight-down-the-legs French-cricket way. Maybe just over someone's front fence. French cricket was just a muck-around before the game.

When it was a proper game they could get a four if they hit a house on the full. A six if they hit a window. An eight if they hit the captain's front door even if the ball bounced. The captain was whoever's house they were playing outside of. When they played on the oval or at the park, the captain was whoever owned the ball. Or sometimes they didn't have a captain. If the ball went straight up the road ahead of them with an on drive or if they knicked it behind them by six car lengths or more, it was a five. And only with tennis balls. If they hit any houses or broke any windows with a real leather cricket ball, they would get caned on the bum or somewhere else from the batter's dad. If he ever found out. If it was George's mum, they would always be found out.

* * *

Inside, Rose and the girls were listening to their American daytime radio serial 'Big Sister' on the wireless set below the mantelpiece; it was up so loud you could hear it in every room in the house.

'Looks good, love. But those scissors look blunt,' Rose said to her eldest daughter.

'They are.'

'Not too long?'

'No, I measured it.'

'George's gotta stone that'll sharpen them. He's got to do my knives too.'

Johnny Want breezed through the living room from the toilet to join his mates on the street playing cricket. He was stopped by Rose.

'Tell George to come in, love.'

'Is he in trouble, Mrs Phelps?'

'He's always in trouble, Johnny.'

'What'd he do?'

'Love, you've got enough trouble in your own naughty bank to buy a small house without worrying about Georgie's.'

'Oh come on, Mrs, what'd he do …'

'Nothing, love, but tell him he is in trouble though, so he comes in. He's gotta try on his footy jumper so I can finish it off. And you better be home before dark today, all right. Your mum says your tea was cold yesterday.'

'Yes Mrs, not gonna miss rabbit stew night. Shot this one myself with Dad. Oh, is George ...'

'Yes, yes, he can go shooting on Sunday. But you know the rules.'

'No carryin' or loading up the rifle till you see the rabbit and me dad has to aim it with him, yes Mrs.'

Johnny was out the door in a flash to join his mates.

* * *

'Bloody beauty!' George let out as he picked the white sun-hardened dog poo off the concrete footpath outside Mrs Anderson's place. 'We got chalk, boys!'

He triumphantly held the cigar-shaped doggie night soil aloft and made his way to one of the two apple-crate wickets in the centre of the street and started to mark the crease with his chalk poo.

Ronnie batted a tennis ball into the crate stumps facing away from the pitch and finally hit a mulligrubber up the pitch to Keithy.

'What's the score again? We startin' new or from yesterday?' Ronnie said.

'Same as yesterday. I'm batting,' George said.

'Start a new one,' Ronnie said.

'You just want a new game 'cause ya got out for a duck yesterday.'

'Big fat golden duck,' Basil added.

'Shuddup. Hit a stone, didn't it,' Ronnie said.

The boys let out a collective 'Oh right!/Balls!/Yeah sure!/Just bad batting!'

'I was aimin' for that stone. Best off spin bowl since Chuck Fleetwood-Smith.'

Johnny interrupted him, running out from the house while he tucked in his shirt. 'Ya mum wants ya, Georgie! Hope it wasn't for the piddle on the loo seat again! She's not that quick, is she?!'

Several boys cried out in unison, 'Yes she is!!'

'Think it's serious, mate. Never know with your mum. What she's thinking. She's nice but, your mum ... She's ... I think you're in trouble, cobber, she's gonna have your guts for garters. Woddya do? Jeez, she's hoppin'.'

'Drinkin' Dad's moonshine, probably. Could be her betting money I took that I was gonna give back. Few to choose from. Might be for killing all his pigeons ... could be ...'

Four other neighbourhood boys joined a huddled circle and watched as a car pulled up and parked one door up.

'Your old man's not in the army, is he? Goldmining in New Guinea, inny? What's a government car doing going into your place?' Ronnie said.

'Probably the war money we're still gettin' when Dad joined up.'

George moved to the house and turned to his mates. 'Start the first over ...'

* * *

Shirley was watching out the window. 'Mum, a man just parked his car out the front and he's looking straight at our house.'

'What's he look like?'

'I can't really tell yet ... Oh, he's in a suit and he's walking straight to our gate.'

'Just one?' Rose asked, her eyes still on her work but her hands shaking ever so slightly.

'Yes.'

'No army man with him. Should be all right, then. Might be bad news if there were two of them.'

'Dad's a goldminer, Mum. He's not in the army,' Joy said.

'Another good thing. Put the kettle on, Joy.'

Shirley watched as the man crossed the back of the makeshift cricket stumps at the bowling end and made his way to the Phelps's front gate and up the steps to the front door.

* * *

The Government Man was ushered into the house and offered a seat and a cup of tea. By the time George walked in, Rose was at the table with his sisters, holding a letter. He entered the room and the bloke stood.

'Mum? What's that?' George said.

'A letter, love. From—'

'No,' he interrupted, pointing to the fabric near the sewing machine. '*That*.'

'Footy jumper. Yours.'

'That's Joy's school uniform! Ya cut the arms off and the dress bit cut up high! And we've got a red V in reps ...'

Joy held up the red V and placed it over the jumper in sort of the right place.

'That's pink!' he scoffed. 'A girl's uniform?! I'll be a bullseye for a bashing!'

'Be thankful and shoosh it now, George,' Rose said, her eyes flashing more of a warning than her words.

The Government Man cleared his throat and extended his hand to introduce himself. 'Hello George. Your mother has told me that I can speak to all of you as a family because she wants you to know as much as possible about what's really going on. Now, your father, he's in New Guinea, son. I have information. There was a Japanese attack on Wau in the north. A surprise attack. The Japs took the place. They occupy it right now. Your dad's mining operation was bombed a month ago – planes in the airfield, houses taken out, a few people were killed. Your dad took off with a group of miners at the urging of our local force. An allied force.' The Government Man paused and made sure he looked into all the Phelps's family eyes. Even tiny Ann, who didn't understand. 'I'm sorry to tell you all the group is missing. We've had no word. I'm very sorry, but they are at this point considered missing and presumed dead. I want you all to know that it is a grave situation and to prepare yourselves for the worst.'

Rose held the letter to her chest, and her daughters started to cry. George's face blanched white.

'We don't know that,' Rose said, her voice strong despite the shake in her hands becoming more pronounced. 'He'll find his way home.'

The Government Man nodded. 'I hope so, Mrs Phelps.'

* * *

'Can you read it, Mum?' Shirley asked after the Government Man had taken his leave.

Rose skipped all the black-ink official titles and 'Office of Origin' and 'No. of Words' and 'Time Lodged' to get to the guts, which she knew was all in blue typewriter ink, all capitals. She made a dainty cough and read: 'IT DESIRES ME TO TELL YOU ...' She looked at her kids one by one, their faces all with the same expression of expectant doom. She had heard the kind firmness in the Government Man's voice when he warned the family to expect the worst, but Rose wasn't ready to give up. And those six words on the telegram were far better than those other six words that began those dreaded telegrams. Oh God. Those six words she had seen on telegrams of friends with men at war in Europe. The same words she had seen on the telegram informing the Challenor family of her brother Albert's death in World War I: 'WE DEEPLY REGRET TO INFORM YOU ...'

She kept reading: '... goldminer/civilian of Bulolo Thomas Henry Phelps +others expected to evacuate by air via Wau failed arrive designated time STOP deemed missing 50 MINERS+ stop all planes destroyed stop whereabouts unknown stop security cannot divulge places & times STOP further information forthcoming STOP GovMT. reP. will follow with RESIDENT CALL stop sincere sympathy MINISTER FOR THE ARMY.'

Joy went to the room she shared with Shirley, and Shirley followed, both sobbing before they reached the door. Rose picked Ann up off the floor.

George rocked in the dining chair looking at the blank wall. *Sincere sympathy.* That would mean he's dead, wouldn't it? Why would they sincerely sympathise if he wasn't dead? George wasn't sure if the telegram was telling the truth. If the Government Man had been telling the truth. He wasn't sure if his dad was trying to get on a plane to get back to them, but where and what was he doing now? Missing?

It didn't mean the words George kept barking at his mother: 'Presumed dead! Presumed dead! He doesn't know that! They don't know that!' The extra bit that was tagged on to the telegrams of soldiers George knew; the bit that meant there was no chance your father/son/husband would survive and the only thing missing was a body.

That evening Rose explained to them that the message didn't mean the worst. She told them their daddy loved them so much he would do anything and everything possible to get out of the way of bad things.

'He got out of the way of the planes that were bombed,' Rose said, 'and he will keep doing that and get back to us.'

CHAPTER 20

The 60 Miles on the Sandy Hoof

'moviaw (Moveave) arrived here by canoe on 20/3/42 at 2.30 pm'

'After one night's rest here we travelled 60 miles down beach by foot to Pinupaka,'

Entry on Tom Phelps's mud map.

Tom and the others couldn't believe their eyes when the Mission rescue party turned up, with others following on the long canoes from the Terapo Mission and the surrounding river village of Moveave. Yet again, the carrier bois had saved the waitmen. The enterprising angel paddlers had come to the fore and they would also go on to collect the rest of the miners, still making their way down the river, and take them to the sea. The bois would do all this on what was foreign soil for them and risk their own lives to get a bunch of waitmen to safety.

The priest left them in the hands of their bois and turned his launch back up the river to help the others still coming.

For Tom it was the entrance to one world, the exit from another; for a moment anyway. It wasn't announced, not even by one of the bois. They had come round the last long bend in the river so slowly and calmly that a few of the blokes in the four canoes were asleep. For the last few miles the paddles had caressed the water only every thirty seconds or so, making the rhythm of the river and paddle a soothing release. They had left the island in the river a full-day back. With that the ever-present sense of dread coming at them round the next tangled vine had receded. Even though they were now on the open wide river with no cover and exposed more than ever to air attack, fear had dissipated for some, on Tom's canoe at least, because it was the longest time they'd had from the last Jap flyover. Maybe the enemy hadn't made it this far south. There was a communal hope that the roughest trot might be over and they were moving further away from what threatened them and travelling closer to what was safe. Maybe even to home.

* * *

The unremitting ride down what they thought was still the Eloa River, but may have become the Lakekamu tested them all. Once saved from the island they had managed to somehow navigate their way around the other rocks that appeared in their path, with sheer luck deciding their fate. The cloying green jungle growth of the Bulldog had made way for the brown river but as they battled the fast-flowing water they still felt closed in. The long canoes they were now in were only really as wide as each man and they lacked gunwales or rails around the sides. The freeboard, which is the distance from the water to the gunnels, was the length of a finger, so any movement aboard had to be minimal, which added to the sense of containment. No one wanted to end up in the drink. They'd seen no sign of the croc – but he had mates. They travelled this final leg of the river on the fashioned flat logs that were virtually flush with the water and they risked capsizing with any drastic movement. Tom's feeling of restriction was compounded by his innate dislike of being a passenger in any vessel or vehicle. He needed to have control, but in this instance he had to relinquish that to the most skilled. And now they'd been saved by the bois he knew he was in the best of hands. They had to trust each other and work to each other's strengths and weaknesses or they'd never make it. Tom was sure of one thing. He wasn't going to die on the

Bulldog Track, and he sure as hell wasn't going to die in a river.

* * *

When the river started to widen and slow, it brought a sense of openness they hadn't felt before. Tom couldn't believe they'd made it. He'd thought the bends in the river would never end.

None of that mattered anymore. Ahead of them was open ocean, the Gulf, the bottom of New Guinea. None of them had seen a watery blue horizon for years. Bloody hell, Tom thought. There's the world and over that horizon, home sweet home. If the canoes had kept going in their southerly direction the Aussie boys knew they would hit the red home soil of the Top End. A forty-five-degree steer to starboard and the closest bit of Australia was waiting for them at Cape York. Saying it sounded easy, but all knew they wouldn't last half an hour in open water in the sheer-to-the-water planks on which they sat. Still, they had survived the first part of the bloody jungle and hopes had lifted, even if bodies ached and home was a long way away.

There were gentle claps and slaps on legs and quiet whoops of achievement. Dozing blokes were tapped awake. A celebration of anything was long overdue.

The nose of each canoe scrunched onto the beach right where the river mouth bent east and kissed the gulf water. Those who could jumped out while the canoe was still moving and moved to aid those not as strong onto the warm sand.

It had nothing on Bondi, this beach with its charcoal rough sand more like semi-soft crunchy gravel, wind ripples replacing ground swell, which meant no surf waves, but for the men this place was not a destination of fun in the sun, it was a passage of survival. But they all agreed it was a gloriously beautiful sight for sore eyes. Tom sighed as he took his wet, stinking boots off and squelched the sand through his bare toes. He felt like a seven year old at his first day on the beach.

Tom's group had been the first to arrive and they rested up, waiting for the other groups to catch up to them at this point. The men were filthy, ragged, wet and permanently exhausted, even though they had been sitting or lying on a canoe deck for a full day's paddle. But most of the seventeen men could still summon the energy to walk around the sandy river mouth and along the ocean beach. The fifteen native bois walking with them had been looking at the open sea in awe and it occurred to Tom that they may be frightened of this *bigpela* river, the like of which they had never seen before.

There was never going to be an itinerary for this maiden voyage. The democratic decisions of where to go next and how to go about it rested with powers beyond a single man; it was down to real-time circumstances, or villagers' local knowledge, or Mother Nature calling the shots, or the decisions of the blokes ahead who were clearing the way for the group's transit forward. There was no discussion about this being the end of one leg and the beginning of the next. They knew from the start of this lark that to get home, it was always going to be the long way round and that at some stage it would be a return to their first mode of travel. They were going to go back on the hoof along the beach. It was pretty much decided after they gathered around the map that their destination of Port Moresby lay to the east.

The lack of barefoot prints in the sand told them little. It was no use asking the highland bois anything about this leg – this coastal terrain was more foreign to them than to the whitefellas. They were looking at this place like the miners first looked at Bulolo.

They looked across the coast from where they had pulled the canoes up to the sand. As far as they could see along the endless stretches of beach, which went in and out of view like a series of boomerangs laid out before them. There was only about twenty feet from the sea tide line to where the solid earth and tussocky bush lay.

The beach they were about to walk on that wound east was the start of the next stage in their journey. For a while at least they were leaving the wet darkness of the jungle where the sun rarely pierced the overhanging canopy of lush rainforest. Tom thought that a blessing. He'd had enough of the feeling of damp that made every step uncomfortable. The cold nights. Clothes had chafed, socks had stuck to blistered skin and the sound of rain had echoed in his ears as he walked up ranges and down valleys and then did it again and again, always another ridge, another mountain ahead. The beach, conversely, was relatively flat and, better yet, the sun found a way to shine. To rest was the most important thing, though. Tomorrow they could start their march onwards, but for now there was fish and coconuts to eat and an overnight bivi. The splintered group, who had come down the river in no uniform fashion, all met up on the beach and so they were able check how others were faring. Tom wrote up the latest instalment on his helmet and realised once he'd recorded 'reached Papuan coast' that there was going to be little room left on the thing to document what had to be further lived.

CHAPTER 21

Bulolo at the Flea House

It was just the two of them on this Saturday arvo. George was with Johnny Want at the flicks. The owners called it the Regent, but no one else ever called it that. It was the Flea House to everyone in the western suburbs; much less posh than the Astoria on Breust Place, a short walk up Acacia Avenue from George's place. It was a special treat to come to the movies with his mates. He wasn't allowed to go alone yet, but at least he didn't have to be escorted by Mum or Aunty Hilda, and it felt good that a lot of the time he could pay his own way from money earned doing odd jobs and the pocket money he got – taken from his dad's goldmining wage – for work around the house.

They'd come to see a cowboy flick double header, *The Cowboy and the Blonde* with *Last of the Duanes*, both starring George Montgomery. Neither boy had ever heard of the actor, but it didn't matter who was in the movie or what it was about. They came because it was the flicks and it was Saturday afternoon.

The last of the three cartoons was the best one because it was a Looney Tunes Daffy Duck. The other two were Inki, the sad crow that never spoke, and a Merry Melodies one with American soldiers. Even the cartoons were full of soldiers. George didn't find any of his favourite cartoons as funny as they used to be. Maybe as soon as you hit the birthday that had 'teen' after it, things weren't as funny anymore. Maybe it was because it was the one where Daffy doesn't fly south and go to war with the other ducks on the pond and instead almost gets eaten for dinner by a wolf and a weasel. George knew that if his dad was alive he would be coming back to his family, running away from the war in the land of the cannibals.

George felt impatient as the projectionist put the newsreel into the projector. Things had changed, and now his focus was less on the cartoons and more on the serious stuff. He wanted any information he could get about New Guinea. He experienced the same mixture of heightened feelings whenever he saw a newsreel with Australia or Australians in it. Abandonment. Fear. Anger. Longing. Love. Loss. Were these all part of what was growing inside him? His whole body felt like an empty hole with the centre in his stomach, a hole he wanted to fill but no one or nothing could do that. Were men of the house allowed to feel like that?

Sometimes one emotion came to the surface more than the others, and sometimes George didn't know how to describe the way he felt even to himself. Not that he ever wanted to talk to anyone. The emotional soup inside him was hard to stomach. Anger had definitely been the strongest and most constant state in those first few months of his dad being away. But now, it was fear.

Still, the Saturday arvo ritual of going to the movies with his mates was hard to beat.

Johnny and George simultaneously chucked a chocolate-and-caramel cobber up in the air and simultaneously scored a mouth goal. Yes! They were about to have another go when he heard it.

'The unique town of Bulolo.'

It was the familiar plummy-mouthed man's English-styled voice, and his first sentence launched George out of his chair with a call of, 'Dad!'

Johnny said, 'Watch it, watch it, sit down.'

'It's Bulolo! Yeah, he said Bulolo!'

He had never heard anyone outside his mum and sisters say the word 'Bulolo', and had only ever seen it on paper in his father's letters when he wrote about his town in the jungle – but it didn't look like a jungle in the newsreel on the screen in front of George now.

'Every single thing that went to build it was flown there. It was destroyed from the air too.'

A bomb-shattered house. Soldiers checking the wreckage.

George whispered loudly: 'It was destroyed from the air, whah? The whole town? There's houses there, not destroyed, you saw those houses yeah? Might be Dad's.'

George was glued to every word and image and never took his eyes off the screen.

'Bob Nesbit had his house there. He used to pan the rivers for gold. Now he's home again. A New Guinea Volunteer Rifleman looking at all that the Japs have left of it.'

He was a miner now a soldier, this Bob on screen. He'd know where George's dad was. Is this what the army man meant when he said 'presumed dead'? Did his dad get blown up in his own house? C'mon, show us the miners. Not just soldiers again. Where's Dad? George got the 'missing' but would not accept the 'presumed dead' from the telegram.

'Bob Nesbit has a big score to settle. He's got something to fight for. Like a lot of other men, he has a family to think about. This is his war, he has a personal stake in it.'

On screen, an upturned rocking horse with, George thought, bullet holes in it. Pictures of kids on the wall.

A miner had a family with kids in Dad's town? George didn't know this. Dad didn't tell him this.

Plummy voice: '*When [the] patrol set out, they had to fight the jungle, to get to grips with their enemy. They plunged through gold-bearing creeks, climbing, slipping, tumbling and pushing on to Salamaua.*'

Soldiers, all with big rifles and all going somewhere. One with a beard slipped and fell sideways on a rock in a stream. Where are the bloody miners?

'*Get off the track and a Jap Tommy Gun is likely to cut you in two. There it is right down below on the narrow neck of land! That's Salamaua.*'

Is that where my dad is or has a Jap Tommy Gun got him?

Soldiers. These three wearing headdresses with grass spikes that stuck straight up, with long, weird Ned Kelly beards. George stopped his loud whispered questions, not because he knew Johnny wouldn't have the answers. He knew that his dad wasn't going to be on this newsreel, or any other. Only soldiers were captured on film.

'*Every move by the Japs there is carefully watched. A ten-thousand-ton enemy transport still burning as a result of a direct bomb hit. Patrols have been at this for weeks, perched up there noting everything and reporting back to headquarters.*'

The jungle from the air. Millions of trees. He thought his dad would be able to stay away from any trouble with all that cover. And wherever they were, soldiers like the ones always on the newsreels would look after their fellow Aussies; that was their job.

'Officials piece together the information that the scouts have turned in. When the battle blueprint is complete, the Australians launch another drive against the Jap positions.'

George thought of his dad's bush-bashing skills and hoped he was with maybe a bushie or two. His dad always said, never go bushwalking alone. Three or more is better, and always tell someone where you're headed. George hoped like hell his dad had carried out his own order.

'Over the wide mountains wrapped in a dense jungle growth, [where] *the sun cannot penetrate, fly the big transport planes to Wau and Bulolo. The aerodromes there are of vital importance to the Allies fighting in New Guinea. Once it was gold dredges, mining equipment and prospectors. Now it's ammunition, guns, food and reinforcements. Diggers for gold yesterday, diggers for Japs today.'*

'Diggers for gold yesterday.' 'Once it was ...' Plummy-voice was talking about George's dad as if all the goldminers had turned into soldiers who were going to dig up Japs. As if his dad and the other non-soldiers had disappeared off the face of the planet. Gold dredges, mining equipment and prospectors replaced by army stuff. It sounded like his dad was going to be swapped for a 303 or, even bigger and better, a Bren gun.

'The flying artillery, twenty-five pounders from the mainland, are flown in sections, to an island six times the size of England. The gunners break records, fitting them together and dragging them into position. The defence of Wau aerodrome is part of their job. Every Japanese effort to take it is met by determined fire.'

It was on with the Japs. Very big guns were shooting up at their planes and spilling crossfire over the town. Huts and houses were exploding. George hoped like hell his old man was nowhere near any of this beause he was alive somewhere.

'They're getting it, from upstairs as well. Those fighters are strafing the Japs good and plenty. That flag was scheduled to fly over territory conquered for Hirohito. Well, the flag's there. That's all. A few of Bob Nesbit's cobbers. Australians stuck out there, with the toughest kind of war on their hands and fighting it like hell.'

He was seeing the ruin of his dad's town. His dad had written to him about it, there was no place like home, he'd said, but he liked it there. George had never felt further away from his father. He had never been sadder in his life.

CHAPTER 22

Angabunga Meets Pinupaka

'... *thence by Lak-atoi to Yule Island ...*'

Entry in indelible ink on
Tom Phelps's mud map.

ARR AT CAMP ON RIVER

Entry with carpenter's pencil on
Tom Phelps's pith helmet.

The second day into the beachcombing leg was clear, sunny, with a warm tropical breeze coming from home over the horizon to the south. It was the same as it had been the day before. It seemed to Tom that in the last hundred miles of black sand prints there was only the constant shooing sound of the windswept surf. No one in the raggedy band of beachcombers had any words to say. The whitefellas dragged on mostly separate from each other, the black sand that never stopped underfoot, the steps on and on that felt as if their feet sank further in the sand every few hundred yards. But it was only over the last few miles that Tom had drifted out of conversation and out of step with his former housemate David Bone, the two who walked the beach together. The only thing shared now was the fatigue and nausea that was doubled by their malaria. There was no medication left for the malaria or any other ailment; they had run out back at the Bulldog camp. For at least six of the seventeen blokes the stopping and bending over to vomit had increased down the river and across the sand. There were just as many stops for those with dysentery and diarrhoea. It was hard to judge or guess anything with the kind of exhaustion and pain that played tricks in his head. Every other bloke would have to have felt the same or worse but they all kept pushing on.

Tom's fevered mind took him far from the beach, his thoughts turning to his wife, his bed at home and the comfort of holding Rose as they lay together on a soft mattress. He wanted to be held in her arms and sleep the deepest, longest sleep a man could have. As his mind wandered he stop noticing the agony of his sandy steps and cramping calves.

He had kept to the rear of the group, walking in the same little random sphere of blokes for no real reason since the Lakekamu river-mouth stage, and for the first time he saw at least a half a dozen of the carrier bois, until then their indestructible angels, stooped and moving at the same snail's pace as the miners. It wasn't out of sympathy for the white men, slowing to keep pace; they were human, and they were just as buggered.

Beyond the bois, about a quarter of a mile up the beach, he noticed the leading mob had stopped and gathered. Ah, rest. Sleep even. On the hot black sand.

But maybe not. He made out a group coming towards them. Locals coming from inland along the beach of another wide river mouth, over low sandhills through a regimented coconut grove then knee-high bush thickets, onto the sand spit to merge with the group. The body language as the last of the trekkers trod the shoreline suggested a peaceful exchange; engaging even. Obviously this coastal mob had seen and dealt with the waitmen before.

Tom and the last lot of the trekkers quietly shuffled onto the sand spit where the gathering took place, a little pencil of sand jutting out like a natural jetty delineating river from sea. It looked like every bit of sand strip they'd seen over the past days, but this one ended in the full stop of a delta.

The way forward would be decided by another committee meeting. An essential-for-survival meeting because each man needed to be on the same page in order to look after himself and watch the back of another bloke, just as they had done all the way down.

Tom pulled out his mud map, knowing that the final entry on the parchment paper was probably going to be somewhere near to where they had landed, because the map had run out of room. It was nearly the same with the helmet, even with his chippy-pencil entries getting smaller and smaller. The map was about the length of the pencil and he kept it in an inner pocket with the indelible-ink pen. It was holding up well considering nothing was ever truly dry. All entries were still legible despite whitewater rapids, sliding down mossy wet slopes and the friction caused by thousands of steps and strides and leaps for days on end.

He unfolded the thirty-two rectangles, wrote his latest note and then folded it back up. There were no maps of where they had trekked so far. The army map they had was devoid of any markings from Edie Creek to the Coast except for the Terapo Mission and the Bulldog abandoned mine. Una Beel told Tom, that he and his fellow miners were the first white men to walk the whole track, others had only ever been to the old Bulldog mine or to the

Mission up the river. He said there were sure to be some villagers along the trek who had seen the waitmen for the first time, but that he wouldn't have been able to see them. They'd have wanted it that way. Tom hoped that if he made it out in one piece, he could show his family – everyone – the map and the inscribed helmet and tell them what he got up to while he was away. And if he didn't make it, then they'd still know.

* * *

All the waitmen gathered around to listen to the local men who had met them on the sand. The old fella in a Western shirt, khaki shorts and missing two front teeth – clearly the elder of the group – was speaking in a pidgin delivered slower than Tom had heard before; Tom still couldn't catch most words, but he got the gist. Port Moresby was being smashed by bombs from probably the same planes that hit Bulolo. A couple of other villagers piped in, and though some words were familiar, most were lost on any of the bois. Port Moresby being bombed was all the info they got about the war, but despite this they decided to press on.

They were at a junction where the river met the sea and a few huts. A short distance over the water in the direction they were heading to Port Moresby was an island. They were close enough to see a few structures and a wharf over the water. Neither the miners nor the bois knew the names of the places they had reached, only that it would be the end of another stage of their journey. How many stages there were still to go on the journey, they were unsure.

The old fella gesticulated descriptively enough that Tom got the name of the river, the man's village and, Tom thought, the island. He heard 'Angabunga', 'Pinupaka', 'Yule misin', 'Jisas'. And he had heard the name of the sail craft from stories in the club in Bulolo. The traditional sail boats were called *lakatoi* – the old bloke repeated this word as he pointed to a horseshoe cove of the river. The group walked together until they saw a row of ten small boats and a large one on the sand.

'*Lakatoi bringim waitman misin. Lakatoi lakatoi. Kingdom bilong Jisas.*' He repeated it again and ended with a laugh, as if he had just told the best gag they would ever hear.

Una Beel translated most of what Tom could tell was local knowledge being imparted from the elder. The sailing boats would take them to the Catholic mission on the far end of the island. There would be no dissenters there. There were men who needed levels of healing and help that a mission with the attendant medical aid and rest would provide. And behind them they hoped other men would soon arrive, men who had started on the track after them, with the same needs coming down the cloud forests and streams in the days and weeks ahead.

Port Moresby was as far away again as they had combed the beach from the Lakekamu river mouth. Centuries away for these fishing folk, but close enough for the canoe telegraph to know what was going on, who was friend and who was foe and what would be the best for these men from another world.

'*Wokabaut pinis, bos.*' Tom didn't need Una Beel's English translation to know that the long walk was over. He knew the meaning of 'wokabaut', the derivative of the Aussie 'walkabout', and like so many pidgin words that came from Australian English it made him smile at its simple, funny ingeniousness. To move on the feet. Wander on foot. To walk.

It made sense to Tom. *Wokabaut pinis, bos.* The literal meaning that the walk had finished right where they were. It was a water journey from here.

The NGVR had issued each miners' party leaving Bulolo with a gulf coastal map as part of their kit – it could very well have been joined up with Tom's first edition hand-drawn map like a jigsaw piece – and Tom had studied the route several times as they rested along the track. The distraction was what he needed back then to fuel the hope that they would make it out and make it home. In his mind's eye now, he saw that the next part of the journey was over water and he felt joy to be getting away from the jungle, the mosquitos, the crocodiles and the slipping and sliding on moss and through mud.

Una Beel was a practical man; innately logical and a quicker learner than Tom thought he could ever be himself. The carriers, once the labourers, the house boys and friends to many of the miner outsiders, were an organic part of everything in their New Guinean existence. Una Beel had only just learned the name of the village behind him, that of Pinupaka, and he knew what must happen next.

'*Wokabaut pinis, bos.*' It was only when Tom heard Una Beel repeat this and saw tears fall down his cheeks and cascade through his whiskers and over his beaming mouth that Tom realised that the *wokabaut* really had ended. Tom swallowed and felt the lump form in his throat. Jesus. What was this feeling? He still wanted to make creations of wood and hike the surrounds of his highland home with Una Beel. Teach him and the other bois how to throw a cut-out pass and be handy rugby league players. Something he had grown used to doing with, yes, his mate. Why here? He never envisaged arriving together at

Central Station with his house boy and Rose making up a bed in the garage for him at Acacia Avenue – but, this? He knew that Una Beel had family, a wife and kids waiting for him in his village just like the others. Of course he was going to go home.

The realisation spread through the group that the bois from Bulolo were saying goodbye to the white men they called '*masa*' and '*bos*' and '*bigpella*'. The men in lap-laps and bare torsos turned the way they had come and walked back along the shore, this time with no sacks or bundles or waitman things. Everything they had with them was theirs. No bois looked back.

CHAPTER 23

Handmaids of Our Lord

'ARR AT MISSION 5PM'

Entry in pencil on Tom Phelps's helmet.

'... where we were for fifteen days ...'

Entry in indelible ink on Tom Phelps's mud map.

The seventeen miners could all fit on the largest lakatoi along with two native crew and captain at the tiller. Other locals surrounded them in smaller craft with two, three and four men and boys aboard them. A slight breeze in the direction of their island destination drifted onto the men's faces and the speed of the craft on the water was a pleasant glide. Some ate the bananas and balls of sago the Pinupaka women had left the men in a pile on the sand. More than half of them had their tobacco tins out and were in the process of rolling up gaspers. Tom had caught the captain's eye and said a 'tenkyu' shortly after they pushed off the sand and he immediately sensed the pride this man oozed as he gave the familiar red-toothed betel nut smile and looked over his bizarre cargo of white, filthy, bedraggled waitmen. As soon as the women placed the banana leaf trays of food down they'd left. They had finished their women's business; the men would carry on with theirs.

Scattered cloud, gentle breeze, good company, tour guides and an island destination. And no more bloody walking! Though many were sick with fevers, or dysentery, or ulcerated blisters, or just physically and emotionally exhausted, they all settled in on their mission-bound flotilla, and to Tom it seemed almost as if they were on a lovely Sunday afternoon cruise on the harbour. If it weren't for every bloke's particular ailment and pain level and the fact that they all still feared attack or death by some other malarkey. But the reality of the situation still weighed heavily. The truth was, they were a long way from home.

Tom was shocked back to that truth when he rolled up his trousers. He could now see bone through the skin of his shin. His personal little volcanoes weren't little anymore, and the word 'gangrene' kept creeping into his head. Doc Giblin did all he could do but couldn't give him what he truly needed, rest.

Tom was glad the chatter on board was of each bloke's connection to the beaches and ocean back home. They'd shared a lot, these blokes, and at times around the campfire they'd all spoken of their lives, comparing what their kids got up to. It urged him on, gave him that little kick to make it through. It made things feel normal when they were far from it.

Despite frailties all round they had become a solid group. None were angels, a few you never talked to much, a couple you couldn't work out, but the seventeen of them had, with the bois' consultation, always talked over their next move and whose needs were greatest. They'd looked out for each other. With every random thing that came their way, whatever happened on the track, it was always a democracy. If it was the seventeen on a lakatoi, or when they split into fours and fives and sixes down the river, or a couple on the hoof, you would try to save another bloke's arse if you could, and you would try to save your own arse too. But you knew you had the other bloke's back and he had yours.

Once again, as they sailed to the mission they could only speculate about what lay ahead. The Japs had wiped out a town of defenceless goldminers simply because Bertie

Heath's plane led some Japs to Bulolo, and they bombed the shit out of them. You couldn't speculate what would happen after that any more than you could speculate what was going to happen from here on in. Gear up for anything. That's what had got them this far. Every inch forward was a new and shared experience.

The lakatoi had a catamaran-type double hull of hollow, sealed logs over which lay a deck of woven vine and kunai grass matting. The sails were tightly woven sheets of fine, tough grasses stitched together and fashioned into U-shaped frames that looked like crab claws and were adjustable to suit wind conditions in a 180-degree horizontal or vertical alignment.

'I'm as thankful as all Christ to be on it, but how do these goddam things stay on top of the water?' queried the big American Jim Hargreaves, who, unlike everyone else aboard, appeared to have lost no weight at all.

John Lovett was standing, holding the mast, 'Bad luck to bring bananas on a boat, isn't it?' he said.

'Rich bloody yachties'll tell you that. They got the luxury of that wive's tale,' Col Phillips said. 'They say that to show off. Makes 'em feel like they're true-blue sailors.'

Bill Warren stood up on the bow holding onto what looked like a bamboo fish trap and turned to his comrades. 'Ah, there it is, boys. That briny air. Reminds me of weekends roamin' round Collaroy and Long Reef. Prawnin' Narrabeen Lakes with me old pop.'

Bill was nearly always up the front of the troop and was the youngest of the lot of them. Tom couldn't remember Bill saying much at all on the trek but his welcoming outburst elicited some smiles of reminiscence and a few head tilts back and intakes of breath through noses to taste the familiar, or not, salty air.

'Can't smell a fucken thing, never could much. Grew up next to a pesticide factory,' Kel Austin said.

'Casino, New South Wales, mate. If it was cowshit I was smelling I'd get all misty eyed,' said farmer Wally Head.

Lofty hung over the water and did a bushie's blow, hoiking snot out of his nose with a thumb over one nostril, then the other. 'We'd go prawnin' every time there was a run up Sussex Inlet way. Holdin' the torch in one hand the net in the other with me dad and pa.'

Tom sat on a fish trap and offered, 'Blackfish off the rocks and walls with a bucket of green weed. Best in winter.'

'Yeah, like me darkies too, Tom. You're Sydney, aren't ya, mate?' John Lovett asked to a head nod from Tom. 'Got a few little spots around the harbour. They don't mind prawns either, the darkies ...'

And so went the comforting banter between the men. The to-ing and fro-ing of the contributions in rhythm with the lakatoi's easy dips over the small swell cruising close to shore.

'Is it Christian this mission or what?' asked Jack Hill as they rounded the easternmost point of the island and several white plantation-style dwellings came into view.

Figures wearing what they could see was black and white attire stood in a line on a jetty, like stumpy lighthouses. A winding path three-football fields long led up to the church on top of the hill, circled by coconut trees. It was in keeping with the Church's ancient, lofty concept that the church or cathedral and its steeple must be the highest point in the town so that everyone could see it and the bells would peel out over all the other roofs to bring people to prayer. The inhabitants of Yule Island didn't need the bells and the highest piece of ground to find their church. The mission was a part of their home. They could find it with their eyes closed.

'Catholic yeah. Kingdom of Jisas, remember the old fella's gabber,' said Wally Head.

'Didn't get a fucken word he said, funny old bugger but,' said Kel.

'He was like a black Charlie Chaplin. Made you laugh without hearing any words.'

'Thought it might be Lutheran with all those Germans running 'round here years ago. Or them Seven Day Adventurers, you got them everywhere,' said Jack.

'They'll have nursing sisters, thank God,' said Doc Giblin. 'And medicines.'

'A bloody bed. Whenever I did get a sleep, I'd be dreamin' of a bloody bed', said Snowy Tomsett.

Doc Giblin added, 'I doubt they'll have enough beds for those on this boat, let alone the ones behind us. There are quite a few houses thereabouts though, so ...'

'It's called Sacred Heart Mission. French Catholic. Just like the Terapo one,' Tom said, interrupting the Doc, who didn't mind. 'We had a priest, a missionary, come to our school one day and he gave a talk to the whole school. Saint Joseph's. All the nuns and priests at this mission come here by ship from Sydney via their headquarters in Paris. Notre Dame. The headmaster musta lined him up through the church brass. And no he didn't have a hunchback ...'

Tom, drawing on the information he'd learned when he'd toyed with the idea of going into the seminary, gave them a few more bits and pieces in his very short history lesson before they got to the jetty. How it was the first home of the Catholic Church in New Guinea and how the French Bishop, who was most likely still there, as missionaries often tended to make a place their life-long home. How he'd started up a new congregation of nuns with local native girls who'd felt the calling as children growing up around the mission. 'The Handmaids of Our Lord.'

'Sacred heart my arse', Tom said after the lesson, not at full volume but not caring if anyone heard him. He couldn't shake the bitterness he felt and couldn't reconcile a supposed sacred heart of a God or Mary or the Lord and His representatives on earth with the cold heart that could take away a baby boy he had barely held in his arms or a young girl who had only just started to speak. What kind of sacred heart could drive his flesh and blood to desecrate the grave of a child?

Tom was as grateful as any of the men on this journey for the rescue and aid from the Terapo missionaries when they saved them from the sand island they had been trapped on, bringing with them food and canoes, when everything appeared lost. But it was too much a pull of his heart to stay in the mission on the Lakekamu. It would be a betrayal he had thought at the time. But on the island they were to step foot on, practicality would take precedence over any animosity towards the Church. He would be no good as a father and husband dying of resentment.

Five startling figures stood out at the end of the rock and earth jetty. As they sailed closer, Tom saw four black faces and one white. One was a native man in a lap lap at the land end of the jetty, standing near a wooden dray hitched to a donkey. The other four were nuns, the Handmaids of Our Lord, no doubt.

'That'd be them there on the jetty wouldn't it, Tom? Jeez we're being saved by bloody penguins,' Lofty, an avowed atheist, said.

The four women had their hands clasped in front of them as they watched the approaching vessels. The black veils under the white caps and the large, round white neckerchiefs gently moved in the sea breeze. Against the blue sky and the green of the island they were like sirens on the rocks in reverse.

In Greek mythology the sirens on the rocks were the dangerous female creatures with beautiful song that no sailor could resist who lured them to their shipwrecked doom onto rocks. The siren nuns on the jetty would not lead the men to their doom, they meant healing and safety and rest. As each group of miners arrived on that jetty in exhausted waves the nuns would nurse every man of every denomination and faith and lack thereof. They would clean and dress every wound, attend to any ailment and assist the priests in spiritual counselling.

The Society of the Sacred Heart of Jesus of Issoudun had established the mission in 1885. Alain-Marie Guynot de Boismenu arrived there in 1897 and was made Bishop in 1900. He had founded new Congregations for Indigenous women in the Handmaids of Our Lord and for native men in the Little Brothers of The Sacred Heart.

The small, smiling man with the long, white Jesus beard and round thick spectacles had run the Missionaires du Sacre-Coeur for forty-two years when the men arrived. He was a deeply devoted and much revered father to all. Like the nuns and priests and locals he nurtured, he would see to every miner.

While he was at the mission Tom would often see the Bishop walking the five mile long and one and a half mile wide island in his ankle-length black robe, pendants and beaded necklace with groups of recuperating miners. He'd listen to stories of the men's epic trip and share tales of mission life across New Guinea and beyond with them all.

During their weeks of respite, many of the miners pitched in to help around the mission and the village, carrying water from the permanent spring, fishing with the locals and kicking a ball around with the kids who called the mission their home.

Boismenu and the people of his mission had known the men were coming. The Bishop told the Bulldog trackers of how the Australian authorities, the military and the government, had given gag orders to war correspondents and others who had gotten wind of the couple of hundred old miners making a trek over uncharted country and the orders to keep shtum to protect them. The Japs had been intercepting radio transmissions and were indiscriminately attacking non-military targets, such as merchant and hospital ships and residential areas. And, as they already knew, mining towns.

It was also believed that a few native personnel had become carriers and informers for the Japanese. That information sent a shiver down Tom's spine as there were still blokes coming down the track. But Tom alo knew the good men who had helped them and so struggled to believe this was true.

The need to keep the men's trek secret explained why there'd been no food and supply air drops along the track. Any biscuit bombs would have painted a big fat bullseye on the travelling bands. It is why no one had been given a radio. They were purposely made incommunicado for their own safety.

Boismenu the Bishop was the conduit through which the military and the native bush telegraph had relayed information, ensuring they kept the miners safe. Villagers had been monitoring the progress of the trackers and any movement of the Japanese as best they could. This local knowledge saved lives up and down the track.

It took Tom half a day spent with Bishop Boismenu to conclude that he did indeed epitomise a representative doing God's work. But it was not enough to erase the memory of a tiny gravestone smashed by his sisters. Nor the girl. The girl on the bike, her body motionless on the road.

This journey he had just made through the jungle and down rivers would always affirm to Tom that mateship, shared humanity, benevolence and family would be his faith. He didn't need to look further than that. He knew because he saw first hand that it was the individual who moulded the good. The individual who looked out for his fellow man. The individual who made a difference. There was no need of a god to do good, and no need of a god to distort that good.

This belief would remain strong for the rest of Tom Phelps's life, even as he called for a priest to give him his last rites on the day he died.

CHAPTER 24

Central

George was only 1052 steps and thirteen train stations away from seeing his dad come back from the dead. The steps were from the first stride from the front gate of Acacia Avenue to the last step into the Punchbowl train station ticket box. On the day of his dad's return, George was going to halve those steps because he was going to run, not walk to the station two streets away. It was the middle of footy season so he knew he could do it fast even in a suit, tie and hat.

He had already gotten up two hours before the sun hit his pillow, his regular alarm clock. He didn't remember if he slept and he didn't care. He knew there was no chance of keeping himself still.

The street lights were still on when he did his dummy run. It was further than he thought – 748 running steps, but it didn't matter, he wasn't actually going to count the steps when the real run happened with Mum and the girls. He'd run ahead to the station and run back to them, then run back to the station. He did this because he couldn't think of anything else to do to fill the time, and the thought of just sitting around thinking about his dad and what shape he was in and even if his dad would remember much about him and the things they used to do together would have driven him crazy. He thought if he ran and ran it might feel like time was compressing, getting closer to the 9 o'clock train arriving at Central Station. The train his dad was on. He sure as hell wasn't going to lie in bed and wait for the whistle of Mum's kettle to get him up.

He was getting his dad back. With Joy and Shirley and Ann. Mum was getting her husband. They were all getting him back. Is that what it felt like for Jesus's disciples when Jesus came back from the dead? Did Mum feel like Mary? When they first got the best telegram anyone could ever get, that lightning bolt of joy and relief. Was that what miracles felt like? That same feeling that popped into George's body and kept a smile on his face and had him saying 'thank you God' repeatedly. That had Shirley and Joy taking turns to burst out crying/laughing and Mum saying to stop whilst doing the same. And baby Ann just crying because her sisters and Mum were. She was two months old when her dad left for the goldfields. She was now almost three and would be able to walk and talk and get to know this stranger and call him 'Daddy', a word she had only ever said when shown photos of him and coached by her siblings to match the word with the face.

George had been fighting in his head for months with the 'presumed dead' and 'missing' tags. It had been too long. If he was missing but alive somewhere he would have tried with every fibre of his being to tell his family he was okay. George knew that. Unless he was a prisoner of war. Or dead. If he thought any of those thoughts for too long he wanted to cry. It was like the darkest of skies had suddenly burst into the purest blue the second Mum read out the telegram.

He wasn't missing, wasn't presumed dead, wasn't presumed anything. He was real, he was alive, he was coming home. Those were his Dad's words in blue ink, spoken himself to the telegram man who sent it on to the house. The postie had delivered the telegram the evening before his Dad's arrival. George had got it from the postie at the door and was told not to unfold it and read it because it could be bad news. He was terrified until his mum unfolded the paper and he saw her face break into a smile.

'Arriving Central 9am, 14th. Love Tom.'

HE WAS ALIVE!

Joy and Shirley immediately jumped up and down screaming.

'He's here! He's here! Dad's here!' they kept saying through tears.

They knew it was fair dinkum from Dad. No fuss, simple. No dramatic flourishes or descriptions of his surviving ordeals through jungles or fighting Japs bare-handed. Not even 'I'm safe. Come and get me' or details of any kind. His dad was never prone to flourishes and George also knew that you had to pay by the word with telegrams.

* * *

The Phelps girls were finally up and almost ready to go. Joy had gotten Ann dressed as usual and tied an orange bow into her hair, which was almost the same colour. Shirley looked in the hallway mirror and adjusted her hat and put a hatpin in. Mum went from room to room for no apparent reason, muttering times and platform numbers and searching for lost nappy pins. Joy told her more than once that all six pins were in place on her coat and marshalled her to the front door yet again so everybody could leave.

George started his run to the station from the living room and had just passed by the letterbox when his mum called out, 'Wait George! Come back love!' She had the telegram in her hand.

'You can run and get the tickets, George love, but get back here quick sticks, I've made a bit of a boo boo. I'm all over the shop right now. Dad's not in 'til nine tonight, I'm sorry.'

'Oh Mum! Have another look.' Together Shirley and Joy let out an exasperated 'Mum!'

'I know, but no, it's the 9pm train tonight. I told you 9am.'

Things stalled in the Phelps house. George ran backwards and forwards up and down the footpath. He didn't know what else to do. The 'Love, Tom.' meant her man had made it out of some sort of hell and was coming back home, the right time hadn't registered. Even George, in the agonising hours leading up to seeing his Dad, had stared at the telegram with a torch in bed without noticing. He'd spent more time scrutinising the official Post Master General's date stamp just to be sure the telegram was real.

'C'mon here the three of you. School uniforms on, you can go to school now, c'mon, it's a 9pm train.

* * *

George, Shirley and Joy agreed that it had been the longest day at school in history. And every kid and teacher at Belmore Tech and Bankstown East schools knew whose Dad was coming home from the war. That was for sure.

* * *

Rose and the girls took up the train seats that faced each other. Rose had Ann on her lap and Joy and Shirley sat opposite. There were nervous giggles and a shared excitement. Rose reassured them their dad was arriving soon and it was really happening. That he was on a train just like the one they were on, coming the opposite way from the north. As soon as she made it real for her girls, she made it real for herself. Tom really was here. They were physically moving toward each other. She let out a little titter of delight and felt like an excited schoolgirl herself.

* * *

Tom knew he wasn't looking too spiffy, wasn't feeling anywhere near like he wanted to, to embrace the family again. He was in the clothes he had walked the length of New Guinea in and even though they had been laundered at the Yule Island Mission during his recuperation, the shirt and trousers were stained by jungle and river and the mining before that. His skin had a banana-yellow hue, he saw a skeleton wrapped in skin in the train's toilet cubicle and sweat droplets joined up and formed non-stop streams all over his body, like a tap was left running in his pores. He had a wheeze in his breathing that he never had on the track. It started when he was on the schooner *Malaita*, halfway from Port Moresby to Cairns, the ship that made the passage back to Aussie soil possible. The ship he and the other miners who had survived the Bulldog Track were passengers aboard.

Next stop Fassifern. Then onto Wyong and Gosford.

* * *

Seven stops to go. George couldn't sit. He walked the carriages from end to end and back, opening and closing each door. He would have walked to New Guinea to see his dad if he had to.

Next stop Campsie. Then onto Canterbury and Hurlstone Park.

George thought there should be a return express train from Punchbowl to Central for fathers seeing their families for the first time after going missing in the jungle. All the people on the train he saw as he went up and down the carriages – where they were going and their reasons for travelling on this train couldn't be as monumental as his.

Next stop Dulwich Hill. Then onto Marrickville and Sydenham.

Rose wondered how Tom might have changed and in what way. Imagination takes over when you have no news or information about the one you love, especially with the heightened circumstances her Tom would have gone through. She didn't know anything about his time in the jungle. She didn't know if he had been in any battles with soldiers, but there must have been battles just to make it back to Australia. Major struggles not just with getting to safety but with the natural elements and the enemy she saw on the newsreels. She wondered if he would be like those World War I returnees with shell shock, uncontrollably shaking and unable to speak. If he had all his limbs. God forbid. 'Arriving Central 9pm, 14th. Love Tom' didn't give any indication as to his state of health or wellbeing. The words on the telegram weren't even physically written by him.

* * *

The bloody malarial shakes. Tom couldn't hide them, which annoyed him more than any pain he felt. He'd lost four stone and was looking gaunt, he knew that. But he was pretty sure what he looked like wouldn't worry his brood too much.

Next stop Woy Woy. Then onto Wandabyne and Hawkesbury River.

Now it felt like he was really home. It was only for a minute as the train click-clacked over the rail bridge before it entered into the comfortable blur of eucalypts. A turn of the head to the left going over the bridge at Brooklyn, the strip of the majestic Hawkesbury River he had fished a few times and knew snaked up to Palm Beach and Broken Bay and the northern most tip of his city. 'Back in God's own country,' Tom said out loud.

Next stop Hornsby. Then on to Central. Home.

* * *

George wondered what his dad was going to look like. Would he come off the train on a stretcher 'cause the Japs shot him, just like on the newsreels where the injured soldier is puffing on a ciggie with his head bandaged? Was he going to have a beard like those Kanga Force soldiers with grass camouflage crowns in their hair? Will he be blindfolded like the newsreel soldier being led through the stream?

Next stop St Peters. Then on to Erskineville and Redfern.

Rose thought about how the wanderlust might have gotten to Tom. How his adventures might make him reject suburban Sydney and his suburban Sydney housewife and kids. The draw back to villages and people he had gotten used to and the attraction to wander further afield.

Next stop Central and Dad.

* * *

Tom figured he was probably down to what thirteen year old George weighed. Or was his son fourteen now?

He had sensed George's slight resentment in the short phrased letters from him over the three years. His descriptions of footie matches he should have been at and the runs of play and tries he'd scored even though he had to give up backyard coaching to go to New Guinea. But he would play it by ear as to how to deal with anything that came up, and probably the best option was to not say anything about the whole bloody thing in New Guinea to anyone and keep it just around all things family. No need to tell anyone. There weren't any war stories like the boys in uniform would have. Most important of all was to get on with life at home as soon as he stepped off the train.

* * *

Central Station. Platform 2. George had run along the platform to the tunnel exit so as to be the closest he could to the train that brought his dad back to him.

He heard the click-clack of the train on the tracks and the whirring sound of the engine echoing in the tunnel getting slower and louder. When the train appeared, slowing to a halt, George ran back to Mum and the girls calling, 'He's here, this is him!' He picked up Ann and held her close. 'Your daddy's here.'

* * *

The train had stopped but Tom stayed in his seat for a couple of minutes. He felt his heart pound and took several deep breaths. Out of the window he saw a small slice of the platform and he could see no one waiting. What to do if they weren't there? Did they get the telegram? He got to his feet slowly with the aid of his walking cane and made for the door. He slid it open and stepped from the carriage trying not to make his walking stick too prominent, putting it next to him on the platform with his kit bag.

And there they were. Three years after waving them farewell from the ship that took him away from them.

Here were the five reasons he held onto, the reasons he needed to get back home. He stood by the train and held his arms out wide, his smile wider, as he said to Joy and George and Rose and Ann and Shirley that yes, 'I made it, I'm home.'

The three eldest of his children ran to their dad as a unit. George with Ann in his arms. They each found a bit of Tom's bedraggled body to hug. Rose walked slowly to her man, not taking her eyes off the face she thought she may never see again. He was rake thin and she had never seen his cheekbones stand out like they did, but it was all Tom. 'I knew. I knew you'd make it love, I knew it. God we were with you. Hello, love.'

Tiny Ann, in George's arms said for the first time, 'Hello Daddy.'

Epilogue

There are no men of the Bulldog Track still with us, as far as I could find in my research. They were sent on their trek seventy-six years ago because they were considered too old or sick to enlist to fight the invading Japanese. I know there were dozens of miners older than Tom who shared this tale, and if Pop, born in 1897, had lived to see this book published, he would have been 121 years old.

It was my mother's suggestion that, if nothing else, this story is a bloody good yarn. Whether written in the year he returned to Australia or now, it's timeless, she would say. This yarn about an ordinary man who survived extraordinary circumstances, his driving force being to get back alive to his family.

In the telling, I made personal discoveries that plopped in front of me like pearls rolling out of their shell.

I connected with my family and our history like I had never done before.

Papua New Guinea was in our blood, and in a continuing connection to the place, my family moved to Port Moresby in 1966, when I was five and my father was working as a refrigeration and air-conditioning engineer for a firm that was commissioned by the Australian army. I started kindergarten at Coronation Primary in the suburb of Boroko. I always felt that both Dad and Pop had a magnetic pull to PNG, and before I arrived there, my boyhood interpretations of my father's and grandfather's smatterings of conversation about the place added to my already active five-year-old actor's imagination. I conjured exotic jungle adventures, living in trees and swinging on vines to get to a mate's place. Communicating and forming lasting bonds with monkeys and saving wayward daughters (always named Jane) of English hunters.

For the two years my family lived there, we did have a coconut tree in the back yard, and Yandibar, our house boy, did teach me how to climb it and retrieve a coconut and reverse frog-hop down again (my first directed performance), as well as make spears and hunt small animals such as frogs and geckos. But other than these exotic pastimes, our house was smack dab in the middle of cleared-jungle, suburban Boroko, Port Moresby. It was probably more like late 1960s suburban Cairns, North Queensland – except hotter, and decidedly wetter.

Suburban Port Moresby in 1966–68 was more rural than it is now. I remember exploring open spaces, creeks and jungle at the perimeters of our town, out all day till sundown – even at age five – with a mob of kids, black and white, Chinese, all sorts. But no swinging vines, no monkey bonding, and no Janes to save.

I discovered early on that when your Aussie parents transplant to another country, they form, or attempt to form, a mirror existence to back home. Especially when the local society is so very different to what they know from birth. Change and difference is, and was, hard.

Social and sports clubs, shops, churches and all the houses of our suburb of Port Moresby – and, I suspect, every other town in PNG – may have been built with local materials but the ethos behind them was still the same as every town back home, and usually at the exclusion of the indigenous or Asian population. We had workers' huts called 'boy houses' at the bottom of our property where immediate families of our workers and our neighbours' workers lived, but the main native village was, as everywhere, on the fringes of town.

My sister and I used to eat dried and salted prunes and plums and other fruit from the Chinese grocer, apparently to replace the salt that the sweat dripped away and thus preventing cramps – Mum's theory, in the end, correct. Grey and wizened and probably kept out in the tropical sun for as long as I was old, they looked as far from fruit as you could imagine and reminded me of the shrunken heads I had seen in *National Geographic*. Every day I expected to see my own real life shrunken heads appear.

My control experiments proved cramps never happened on the days I sucked on my salty mouth sponges. I didn't tell Mum; didn't need to, because anything shrivelled up and salted rocked my little boat.

It seemed all the shops were Chinese-run. My salty shrunken heads became my favourite lolly and started a lifelong love of all things dried, pickled, salted, rotting, preserved and savoury. It only takes one taste of an extremely saliferous plum and I can go back fifty years to an Asian grocery store and see and smell the Koki Market at Port Moresby's Eli Beach. Remembering fish covered with flies in the baking sun. Everything covered with flies even in the pouring rain. Live and smoked tree wallabies and *cuscus* (possums) in rope baskets awaiting sale for a family's meal.

I recall the first and last time seeing a piglet suckling from a woman's breast, and Mum and Dad's explanation just making it more confusing and weird. Being attacked by the neighbour's pet cassowary. Yandibar, who always wore a bandage on his right knee on Sundays, giving after-school frog-spearing lessons if it rained. Coconut-tree climbing lessons if it was dry. It probably explained the culture shock on returning to Sydney and starting at Newport Public School two years later, and why I had to repeat first class. It wasn't because I flunked plasticine. But it may have been what I thought was my seven-year-old's grammatical and geographical freedom to randomly walk out the classroom door spouting, 'Just having a piss, miss.' It had worked at Coronation Primary, but not at Newport Public. Mum having to come to school and my half-haiku poetry going unrewarded. These socialist leanings and freedoms of speech were eventually expunged from my repertoire once I re-entered the northern beaches of Sydney.

Just as Pop's tenure in the goldfields was violently interrupted by an invading enemy, my dad's tenure came to an early end when his boss did something you never do to any male Phelps, ever. During a public dressing down for something my dad didn't do, the boss repeatedly poked him in the chest. No. That would be a no. Must be in our DNA too. The boss didn't get up for quite some time after the straight right my dad delivered to his bonce. He wasn't really sure how long *masta bos* was down because Dad was already packing up his desk and making mental plans for the family's return to Sydney.

* * *

For the past five years I have lived in the house I was born in. Or, more precisely, the house I was brought to from Manly Hospital as a six day old. My father and grandfather built this house, and in it our daughters have grown from seven and ten to our pride-and-joy teenagers. As I write, my bare feet rest on the pine floorboards that Tom and George Phelps hammered into place and varnished and where I crawled before I could walk.

My own journey writing this story was an intensely personal one. Dad had very clear recollections of his boyhood and he was my expert research go-to guy for those days in 1942. Pop's experience in New Guinea was as a civilian and therefore it was undocumented in the conventional sense. His diaries and anecdotes are woven into our family's tapestry. I also pieced this time in his life together using his entries on his helmet, hand-drawn map and photos as blueprints and guides, and with the help of my father and mother and Tom's eldest child, Joy, with whom Pop would share details of his New Guinea odyssey.

For the remaining three years of the war and for some years after, Tom Phelps helped the war effort by putting his fine carpentry skills to use in the manufacture of plywood planes. He was always in the garage workshop making something beautiful in wood and only stopped when his body wouldn't allow him to go on.

My wife, Donna, and I don't sit on it yet because we think it might make us feel too old, but we have a love seat crafted by Pop Phelps on our side verandah. It was handed down by Mum and Dad and the cats love it in the north-facing sun.

In the early 1970s Tom and Rose moved from Punchbowl to a tiny fibro cottage in Gorokan on the NSW Central Coast, surrounded by lakes and streams at all points of the compass. (I always wanted them to live in neighbouring Budgewoi because it was such a great word.) Tom became a very handy pennants lawn bowler with the Halekulani Club and increased the time spent a thousandfold fishing for blackfish, his favourite pastime. In my teens I would dive around the rock pools and the peak rocks of Newport and Bilgola beaches retrieving the lime-green weed bait when I knew he was coming down to visit, or pack it in plastic bags when we went to see them.

To this day, I continue talking with my ninety-year-old Aunty Joy of her father and brother. She was a Head

Nursing Sister at Lismore Base Hospital for twenty-odd years and still leads meditation classes with mostly retired nurses, writing her own meditative scripts to inspirational music. She runs a coffee plantation in northern New South Wales with her partner of fifty-eight years, Joan. They grow 2000 coffee plants, roast the coffee on site and sell and serve it in their cafe among the coffee plants that my pop, her dad, Tom Phelps, built just like he built his daughter's house across the street. (I edited out 'single-handedly' after speaking to the girls on the phone to get some facts straight and they told me there were labourers on the cafe and the house, sawing and hammering and planing and sweating as much as Tom did.)

Both Joy and Joan are judges of coffee at shows and festivals around the country. They got this gig because they were rated for so long as the best homegrown coffee in the country and won so many Best Coffee Blue Ribbons at shows that the folks in the Australian coffee world that mattered urged them to be twin taste meisters of the beautiful bean.

Only the other day Aunty Joy told me for the first time that after the family walked Tom home from the train station upon his miracle return, they put him to bed and got him a cup of tea and sat around the bed in tears of joy (literally). A cuppa and a good lie down. Just what the doctor ordered after all that walking across a country. Australian penicillin. It worked apparently, and so did the buckets around the edges of Tom and Rose's bed to catch the flowing stream of sweat coming from Tom's emaciated body due to his malarial fits.

Pop would be nursed by his wife, who was known to be a healer of the highest order. Nan Phelps would not let tropical ulcers or malaria or anything adverse bring her family down. She had once refused doctors' insistence on amputating her man's leg. She had told them to get stuffed, and they eventually saved the leg.

I began this book when my father became very sick. In or out of hospital he loved to have his granddaughters sing and read to him and hear some of the latest instalments of the book. Dad and Mum, in their sixty-sixth year as husband and wife, would let me know of any inaccuracies and how they felt as a reader of something that was so personal and even closer to the story than I am; they had lived and breathed it. Just as my wife Donna does daily, their love and encouragement got me over the many humps with a simple, 'It's good, mate, keep going, I just think maybe you should ...' I would nearly always make the changes they suggested.

I got the same sparkle and smile from Dad as when my youngest daughter sang to him or my eldest read to him, so I always took his advice and kept going. I get the same one-line advice from my daughters Aja and Polly whenever I'm staring into space unable to get something on the page, or indulging in some obvious distraction, but it's usually much more firmly delivered and with an exasperated tone. 'Dad. Just *write*.'

I had been scribbling longhand in Dad's palliative-care room, working on the chapter that detailed his father's evacuation from Bulolo, when my mother and I knew from his breathing that he was leaving us. We lay down and held him on either side, talking to each other, 'It's okay to say goodbye,' until he drew his last breath.

Dad's ashes are in the wind and waves of Newport Beach where he swam every morning for years, in all seasons and in all conditions with his mates in the Newport Knackers. He was usually the first one there before the sun came up, the first in the surf. With Dad's wishes I spread his ashes at the paddle-out ceremony in front of the surf club, the ocean embracing Dad's last swim with his old mates and the boys I grew up surfing with.

I delivered this book to my publisher from the headland at Newport. I looked down on the reef and on Kylie, the orange buoy anchored about 200 metres off the surf club where the boys swim out to, and with a 'Here it goes, Dad; off it goes, Pop', I clicked 'send'. I'm pretty sure they both would have said, 'It's all right, mate, do it.' Or, with Dad, it may have been more, 'Hope you've got a good editor.'

* * *

The Bulldog Track became the Bulldog Road and was ranked one of the 'great army engineering feats of history' (General Sir Thomas Blamey). The track that my grandfather and his fellow miners became some of the first white men to cross became the passage that provided a secret overland supply route for Australian forces and was instrumental in the resistance of the Japanese invasion of Port Moresby.

Little did he know but Tom Phelps would be a link in the chain of success at pushing back the enemy. Government and military representatives visited him at home while he was still being nursed by my grandmother. They interviewed him and others who made the trek, no doubt amazed at how these 'unfit for enlistment' men survived the ordeal, and through their recounting of their experiences the army went ahead with the six-month construction of the Bulldog Road. They requisitioned Tom's mud map and helmet, with their dates and times, descriptions of terrain and accounts with the natives. What they had in their possession would be the first blueprints of the road that would be a major factor in the Australian Force's success.

The authorities returned the map and helmet to my grandfather. They are on the table on which I write.

Ernie Tomsett and a few of the blokes who made the 'walk across New Guinea' with Tom called his helmet-and-rice-paper record 'bloody pointless' and of 'no use to anyone', no doubt all in good fun. It would have been typical of Tom Phelps, according to my dad, to give a wry smile, say nothing and carry on. Something he would do his whole life. Something Dad did a fair bit near the end.

In telling my pop and my dad's story I have carried on their legacy and reinforced what is important to me and was to them – family, and a safe place to call home. It is all that matters.

Acknowledgements

My father shared his memories of the time in precise detail and he gave me his blessing to tell this story. I miss you, mate. Thank you to my mother, Shirley Phelps OAM, and Aunty Joy Phelps and Joan Dibden for family history updates and the photos and memorabilia.

Thanks to the staff of the Mitchell Library Special Collections, who guided me precisely where I needed to go.

Thanks Donna, the Spartan warrior mother of our children (medals pending – to her) and our gorgeous daughters, Aja and Polly, for giving your old man the space and time to knock this thing out. Your dad's rantings and vague looks out onto Pittwater to rescue a sentence here and a paragraph there have hopefully translated into a good yarn about Poppy and your great-grandad.

I read that Martin Scorsese's favourite part of the filmmaking process is in the editing room. Like the best film editors, book editors can help shape not so good words into much better ones. When I first received the edits back from Hachette, the publisher of this book, I learned quickly that the process of writing was not so much a solo journey as I thought it might be. My Robinson Crusoe island would have Woman and Man Fridays. I had thankfully acquired a team of caring and insightful folks who would nurture and finesse a trip as unknown as my grandfather's journey across New Guinea. Thank you Vanessa Radnidge, champion, precise, patient and caring person of the word. And Brigid Mullane, your notes helped make the whole thing flow. I would also like to thank Claire de Medici, Jacquie Brown, Tom Bailey-Smith, Caitlin Murphy, Isabel Staas, Fiona Hazard, Louise Sherwin-Stark, Justin Ractliffe, Lydia Tasker, Thomas Saras, Daniel Pilkington, Andrew Cattanach, Chris Sims, Katrina Collett, Graeme Jones, Christa Moffitt and everyone else at Hachette, as well as the booksellers and librarians who have helped connect this book to readers.

References

Brune, Peter, *A Bastard of a Place: The Australians in Papua,* Allen & Unwin, Sydney, 1999.

Flannery, Tim, *Throwim Way Leg: An Adventure,* Text Publishing, Melbourne. 2009.

Huxley, Jim, *New Guinea Experience: Gold,War & Peace,* Australian Military History Publications, 2007, Collection, Mitchell Library, Sydney.

Waterhouse, Michael, *Not A Poor Man's Field: The New Guinea Goldfields to 1942 – An Australian Colonial History,* Collection, Mitchell Library Sydney.

White, Osmar, *Green Armour,* Angus & Robertson, Sydney, 1945, sourced Mitchell Library Sydney.

Australian National University – anu.edu.au | asiapacific.anu.edu.au/pambu

Australian War Memorial – awm.gov.au/trove

National Archive of Australia – naa.gov.au

National Library Australia – nla.gov.au | trove.nla.gov.au

Pacific Manuscripts Bureau – asiapacific.anu.edu.au

Papers Past NZ – paperspast.natlib.govt.nz

Research School of Pacific Studies, Division of Pacific & Asian History.

Thomas Henry Phelps self drawn map, inscribed helmet diary, Phelps family lore.

Peter Phelps is one of Australia's best-loved actors, regularly appearing in film, television and theatre productions. He is an AFI and Logie award winner and has directed episodes of *All Saints* and *Home and Away*. In 1994 he wrote *Sex without Madonna: True confessions of a hired gun in Tinseltown* (a wry look at his years in Hollywood). *The Bulldog Track* is a very personal account of his grandfather's incredible survival in New Guinea during WWII, and his escape by the 'other Kokoda trail'.